Coronaquake Chronicle

how COVID-19 changed everything

Winston C. Fraser

Layout and production: Jim Fraser

Front cover design: Nurdin Musaev

Dedication page photo: author

Back cover photos:
> Top left and top right: istockphoto.com
> Top middle: author
> Bottom: Andrea Fraser

Printed and bound in Canada by:
Katari Imaging
282 Elgin St.
Ottawa, ON K2P 1M3
613-233-1999
www.katariimaging.com

Printed and bound in the USA by:
Ingram Spark (www.ingramspark.com) and others

ISBN: 978-1-7771308-1-7

Dedication

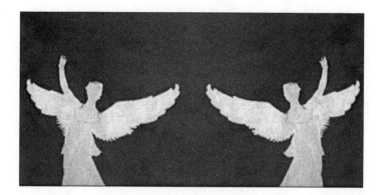

This book is gratefully dedicated to all those working on the front lines of the COVID-19 war – the army of angels acting as lanterns of light, heralds of hope and crucibles of care in the frantic fight to wrestle a merciless monster into silent submission.

God bless you one and all for your dedication and service.

Foreword

Merriam-Webster defines chronicle as "a factual written account of important or historical events in the order of their occurrence."

Winston Fraser has successfully achieved this chronicle in providing his audience with an objective, factual and highly informative account of the impact the COVID-19 pandemic has had on the world. He has carefully documented this tragedy from the first signs of danger in Wuhan to the international crisis that has yet to subside. Pragmatist and realist that he is, Fraser cautions us that, as the future evolves, ". . . we must be prepared for an extended series of aftershocks of unknown magnitude."

Readers will find this chronicle of events well organized and very "reader-friendly." Fraser has taken "a step back" and analyzed for us the events as they unfolded, from the initial social distancing and elbow bumps, to the cancellation of all major sports and the complete lock-down of major cities. He addresses the many areas of our life and culture that have been impacted, including shopping and travel restrictions, "technology to the rescue," "living in isolation" and the "financial frenzy."

According to Fraser, "COVID-19 changed everything." He then focuses on how the pandemic has changed "our world." It is each individual person who is impacted by this world crisis. Without being overly dramatic, pandering or nostalgic, he shares with us stories of how individuals are coping with this total change in lifestyle. Fraser does not try to interpret what his contributors are thinking or to analyze what they are feeling. He simply reaches out to his family and his many friends and colleagues, asking them to share their perspectives about COVID-19. The insights, from such a wide selection of individuals, is a wonderful addition to a book that is already a must-read.

This book will be valued by all who have lived through this pandemic. As well, it will give future generations an insight into what it was really like, as the human race battled the pandemic.

I have great respect for the work of Winston Fraser. He is brilliant, he is authentic. He is humble and he has a great sense of humour. His writing keeps the reader hooked. And last but not least, there is always that ever-inspiring message of hope in his books. This book is no exception. I urge you to read this book and take a moment to reflect on Betty Maine's inspiring reflections in Chapter 18.

"Ça va bien aller!"

> — Jim MacKinnon, retired high school principal, Beaconsfield, Que.

Preface

Shifting gears (istockphoto.com – credit matejmo)

The idea for this book was conceived on March 30, 2020 – the seventh day of my COVID self-isolation. I had just completed the final edits of my new photography book *'scapes to behold – a photographic anthology* and was starting to work on another one. However, I seemed to be suffering from "writer's block" – the words weren't flowing from my favourite Cross pen. Then it suddenly came to me that I needed to shift gears in terms of my literary labours.

As a writer and photographer, I felt it incumbent on me to drop everything else and to document this unprecedented period in our history. So that is why I decided to write a book to record for posterity the enormous impact that the COVID-19 pandemic is having – how our world is literally being turned upside-down. Some have asked me why I didn't wait until the crisis was over. My answer was that I felt it important to document the crisis while we are living through it, before the present perilous period passes into the pages of history. Also, as we all know, memories can be fragile and fleeting. I want people to realize years from now that this situation really **did** happen and that it was not just a bad dream.

To solidify my decision to move ahead with this project, I obtained the concurrence of my trusted sounding boards (my daughter Elaine and my brother Jim). Then I reached out to family, friends and acquaintances to invite them to share their own COVID-19 experiences for inclusion in my book. To clear my conscience of any guilt about personally profiting from the pandemic, I hereby pledge to donate my share of book sale proceeds to the Montreal Neurological Institute Foundation in appreciation of the outstanding care that I have received over the past three years, thus allowing me to continue to function quite normally in spite of my Parkinson's condition.

My only objective in writing this book is to document the COVID-19 crisis, particularly from a mainly personal perspective of a Canadian living in Quebec. It is not to judge or to justify the various actions taken in response to the pandemic. Those aspects I will leave for greater minds to analyze, synthesize and criticize.

As you read this tome, may you stay safe, stay well and stay connected with those you love.

Note: As you peruse the pages of the present prose, don't be concerned by the seemingly random use of the present and past tenses. It's just that so much was happening in real time as I wrote. Please note also that this book was written during the first six weeks of the pandemic in Canada, from mid-March to the end of April, 2020.

Acknowledgements

I wish to acknowledge the invaluable assistance of my family, friends and acquaintances who generously shared their COVID-19 experiences, and in so doing, added a particularly personal perspective to this book. The list of those who responded to my reach out, or assisted in any other way, is long and I apologize in advance to anyone who may have inadvertently been omitted. To all of the following I extend my sincere thanks:

Abdellah Tabarani, Andrea Fraser, Andreas Lazda, Ann Gillard, Art Pease, Barb Ward, Betty MacKinnon, Betty Maine, Bill Ivy, Bob Simon, Bob Taylor, Bruce Singleton, Caleb Beck, Cameron Fraser, Carol Alette, Carol Alguire, Carol Rand, Céline Léger, Charles C. Fraser, Charles W.K. Fraser, Charlotte Taylor, Clare Parsons, David Fraser, David Gussow, Delaney Callahan, Diane Keet, Don Parsons, Dr. Anne-Louise Lafontaine, Dr. Paul Piechota, Dyane Peat, Elaine Fraser, Elizabeth Harvey, Evan Dunfee, Frank Hall, Frasier Bellam, George Dunbar, Ginette Arcand, Glad Parsons, Greg Beck, Gweneth Thirlwell, Harry Bellam, Jacob Lazda, Jacques Crépeau, Jennifer Hurd, Jennifer Tracy, Jim Fraser, Jim MacKinnon, Jim Robinson, Joanne Carruthers, John Thévenot, June Patterson, Karen Jackson, Kennedy Fraser, Kerri Fraser, Kira-Marie Lazda, Larry Diamond, Linda Bergman, Lisa Taubensee, Lorenzo Tartamella, Makeda Smith, Margaret Eastwood, Margaret Gussow, Marilyn Reed, Mattias Lazda, Micayla Beck, Monique Marson Stever, Monique Thirlwell, Nadia Chebki, Niki Underhill, Pat Beck, Pat Ivy, Pat Tracy-Callahan, Ray Hession, Rev. Sophie Rolland, Richard Wilding, Ron Planche, Royce Rand, Sally Aldinger, Sally Harmer, Sharon Moore Rand, Skyleigh Hurd, Steve Fraser, Sue Hartke, Susan Fowler, Tara Abramyk, Tracie Dougherty, Warren Fraser.

I also want to thank graphic designer Nurdin Musaev for his cover design services, artist James Harvey for his sketching expertise, and my son-in-law Greg Beck for his professional photo retouching. Finally, a special word of appreciation to my brother Jim for his expert proofreading, layout and production services.

Contents

Chapter 1
Pandemic perspectives

\# MARCH 2020						
SUN	MON	TUE	WED	THU	FRI	SAT
1	2	3	4	5	6	7
8	9	10	11	12	13	14
Ides of March 15	16	17	18	**Spring Equinox** 19	20	21
22	23	24	25	26	27	28
29	30	31				

For me – and I suspect for many Canadians – the COVID-19 earthquake struck around breakfast time on March 13, 2020. A quick glance at the calendar showed that it was two days before the dreaded Ides of March!

As I was cleaning up from my standard post-retirement breakfast of bran flakes with berries, bananas and stewed prunes, I was suddenly jolted by a news bulletin on CBC Radio One. The prime minister's wife, Sophie Grégoire Trudeau, had just tested positive for COVID-19 and Justin Trudeau himself was now in self-isolation. That announcement made me sit up and take notice. Yes, I was aware that the ground had been severely shaking in other parts of the world, including China, Iran and Italy, but this was much closer to home. I immediately texted my daughter, Elaine, a Montreal school principal: "Justin T's wife has COVID-19." *(Sent at 9:15 a.m. on Friday March 13, 2020.)*

A rapid exchange of texts between us ensued, in which Elaine informed me of an overnight message she had received from her school board: "The Lester B. Pearson School Board has made the decision to close all of its Schools, Centres and Daycares for tomorrow, Friday, March 13th." *(Sent at 10:45 p.m. on Thursday March 12, 2020.)*

Thus began an odyssey that has intensified on a daily basis with no end yet in sight. In fact, our political leaders and medical experts have clearly warned that the situation will get worse before it gets better. In other words, we must be prepared for an extended series of aftershocks of unknown magnitude. Given that reality, we must learn to cope as best as possible. I, like many others (some of whom share their reactions below), had not imagined the extent of the impact.

> Carol and I follow the news, saw what was happening in Wuhan, China, and knew the novel coronavirus was coming – eventually. But, like most of us, we hadn't given much thought as to when or to how it might impact us personally. We had read that healthy people were not particularly at risk. We never, ever considered the possibility of such a large-scale, prolonged societal shutdown! The first significant personal impact was on March 9, when the training course I was scheduled to deliver in mid-April in Munich, Germany, was postponed to an indeterminate future date. (Jim Fraser)

> We came up to our weekend home in Jackson, N.H., for a long weekend on Thursday, March 12, after Sean was told to work remotely, and have been in isolation here ever since. On our drive up, we called our son Liam, a high school teacher in Manchester, N.H. He asked if we were prepared to spend 14 days in Jackson, and said that he and his wife Karri were staying home for the weekend because they feared exposing us to COVID-19. We stopped at a grocery store along the way and stocked up. Things unfolded quickly on the weekend of March 14. Some schools had been ordered closed, then by Saturday, all schools in Massachusetts and New Hampshire were ordered closed. All the mountains were open, then they started closing one by one – by Monday, they were all closed. All of us, except for our daughter Delaney, started working remotely. Luke is studying for his MBA, and all of his classes have moved to online only. (Pat Tracy-Callahan)

In this chapter we provide a chronology of the major milestones of the spread of this extremely serious virus – it is many times more contagious and many times more deadly than the common flu – and of the actions that Canada and Quebec have taken to control/mitigate the contagion. We also cast this crisis in a historical perspective by contrasting it with other major world pandemics that have occurred in the past. Finally we review some of the international missteps that may have contributed to the gravity of the current situation. But first, to put everything in context, we explain some of the medical jargon associated with the infection – both newly coined terms and adaptations of existing ones.

Understanding the medical jargon

The table on the following three pages defines the most common terms associated with COVID-19.

Term	Defintion/explanation
Coronavirus	Coronaviruses are a large family of viruses which may cause illness in animals or humans. In humans, several coronaviruses are known to cause respiratory infections, ranging from the common cold to more severe diseases such as Middle East Respiratory Syndrome (MERS) and Severe Acute Respiratory Syndrome (SARS). The most-recently discovered coronavirus causes coronavirus disease COVID-19. *(source: WHO)*
COVID-19	COVID-19 is the infectious disease caused by the most recently discovered coronavirus. This new virus and disease were unknown before the outbreak began in Wuhan, China, in December 2019. COVID-19 is short for "coronavirus disease 2019," named February 11, 2020. *(source: WHO)*
elbow bump	The elbow bump is a way of greeting each other without shaking hands. *(source: https://www.btb.termiumplus.gc.ca/publications /covid19-eng.html)*
essential services	Essential services are retail services deemed essential to meet the diverse needs of Canadians. The definiton varies by province. *(source: Retail Council of Canada)*
flatten the curve	Flattening the curve refers to community isolation measures that keep the daily number of disease cases at a manageable level for medical providers. *(source: www.livescience.com)*
incubation period	The incubation period is the period between exposure to an infection and the appearance of the first symptoms. *(source: https://www.lexico.com/definition/incubation_period)*
isolation	A measure to prevent the spread of a disease in which the infected person is completely separated from others. *(source: https://www.btb.termiumplus.gc.ca/publications/covid19-eng.html)*
lockdown	An emergency protocol intended to prevent people from leaving an area or defined location. (source: https://www.btb. *termiumplus.gc.ca/publications/covid19-eng.html)*
N95 respirators /masks	NIOSH or equivalent approved N95 surgical respirators are designed to reduce the risk of inhaling hazardous airborne particles and aerosols. These respirators are medical devices authorized by Health Canada. An N95 respirator is a respiratory protective device designed to achieve a very close facial fit and very efficient filtration of airborne particles. The "N95" designation means that when subjected to careful testing the respirator blocks at least 95% of very small test particles. (. . . Cont'd)

Term	Defintion/explanation
(Cont'd) N95 respirators /masks	Medical masks are also medical devices that use materials that block at least 95% of very small test particles, however, they do not fit tightly to the face, so are not designed to provide complete protection for the wearer. Both respirators and masks need to be used in combination with appropriate eye protection (e.g., face shield, goggles) to achieve full protection of the eyes, nose and mouth. *(source: https://www.canada.ca/en/health-canada/services /drugs-health-products/medicaldevices/activities /announcements/covid19-notice-home-made-masks.html)*
pandemic	An epidemic occurring worldwide or over a very wide area, crossing international borders, and usually affecting a large number of people. *(source: https://www.btb.termiumplus.gc.ca /publications/covid19-eng.html)*
peak	Refers to the highest number of cases in a country or region, after which the rate of infection begins to slow. *(source: https://www.summitmedicalgroup.com/news/living-well/must-know-covid-19-vocabulary/)*
physical distancing	Physical distancing means making changes in one's everyday routines in order to minimize close contact with others, including: - avoiding crowded places and non-essential gatherings - avoiding common greetings, such as handshakes - limiting contact with people at higher risk (e.g., older adults and those in poor health) - keeping a distance of at least two arms lengths (approximately 2 metres) from others, as much as possible *(source: canada.ca)*
plank the curve	Planking the curve means taking rigorous measures to drastically slow down the increase in the number of cases of a disease to avoid overwhelming the health care system at the peak of an epidemic. *(source: https://www.btb.termiumplus.gc.ca /publications/covid19-eng.html)*
PPE	Personal protective equipment consists of gowns, gloves, masks, facial protection (i.e., masks and eye protection, face shields or masks with visor attachment) or respirators that can be used to provide a barrier to help prevent potential exposure to infectious disease. *(source: https://www.canada.ca/en/health-canada/services/drugs-health-products/medical-devices/covid19-personal-protective-equipment.html)*

Term	Defintion/explanation
quarantine	A measure to prevent the spread of a disease in which a person who has been potentially exposed to the infectious agent is isolated from others. *(source: https://www.btb.termiumplus.gc.ca/publications/covid19-eng.html)*
self-isolation	Self-isolation is when you have been instructed to separate yourself from others, with the purpose of preventing the spread of the virus, including those within your home. If you are ill, you should be separated from others in your household to the greatest extent possible. *(source: https://www.ottawapublichealth.ca/en/public-health-topics/self-isolation-instructions-for-novel-coronavirus-covid-19.aspx)*
social distancing	Initially synonymous with "physical distancing," this term's use was discouraged by WHO officials at a daily news briefing on March 20, saying that while maintaining a physical distance was "absolutely essential" amid the global pandemic, "it does not mean that socially we have to disconnect from our loved ones, from our family." *(source: WHO)*
ventilator	Mechanical ventilators are machines attached to patients, either via a tube inserted through the mouth and into the throat, or with a tight-fitting mask that goes around the nose and mouth. The machine forces air into patients, providing extra oxygen to support their breathing muscles. This allows the patient to relax and exhale. *(source: https://www.ctvnews.ca/health/coronavirus/why-ventilators-are-so-crucial-in-treating-covid-19-patients-1.4877810)*
vulnerable person	A vulnerable person means a person who (a) has an underlying medical condition; (b) has a compromised immune system from a medical condition or treatment; or (c) is 65 years of age or older. *(source: https://orders-in-council.canada.ca/attachment.php?attach=38989&lang=en)*

Chronology

The table below summarizes some of the major milestones associated with the COVID-19 pandemic.

Some major milestones associated with the COVID-19 pandemic

Date	Action
Dec. 31, 2019	A pneumonia of unknown cause detected in November in Wuhan, China, was first reported to the World Health Organization.
Jan. 25, 2020	First presumed case in Canada.
Feb. 28	First presumed case in Quebec.
Mar. 5	Canada has reported 34 cases in the country so far, and public health officials say the risk to the public remains low.
Mar. 11	The World Health Organization declares the COVID-19 outbreak a pandemic. NBA suspends its season.
Mar. 12	Prime Minister Justin Trudeau and his wife self-isolate after Sophie Grégoire Trudeau tests positive. NHL suspends its season.
Mar. 13	Quebec shuts all daycares, public schools, CEGEPs and universities.
Mar. 14	Premier François Legault asks everyone over the age of 70 to stay at home. Visits to hospitals and seniors' residences are banned.
Mar. 18	Canada and the U.S. announce their shared border will close to non-essential traffic. Canada announces an $82-billion financial aid package to help workers and businesses.
Mar. 19	First death in Quebec.
Mar. 21	Quebec bans all indoor and outdoor gatherings.
Mar. 25	Canada invokes the Quarantine Act.
Apr. 14	Quebec redefines essential services.
Apr. 15	Quebec appeals for additional health care workers for long-term care facilities.
Apr. 17	Quebec requests military help for long-term care facilities.
Apr. 24	Ontario requests military help for long-term care facilities.
Apr. 27	Quebec announces plan to reopen elementry schools on May 11.

(source: https://cmajnews.com/2020/05/15/coronavirus-1095847/)

Historic comparisons

Politicians and reporters are tripping over themselves to find the strongest terms to describe the COVID-19 crisis. Among the adjectives used are: extraordinary, unprecedented, apocalyptic and unparalleled. Not to in any way understate the seriousness of this pandemic, some of these qualifiers frankly fall into the hyperbole category. In fact, from a historical vantage point, this crisis is not unprecedented. In the past 100 years alone, as illustrated in the table on the following page, several other pandemics have resulted in higher numbers of deaths than COVID-19 is projected to cause. But having said that, it is acknowledged that the overall impact of the current contagion could well turn out to be greater than most of its predecessors.

Spanish flu sign (Science History Images/Alamy Stock Photo #HRP0YG)

The table on the following page lists some of the major pandemics that have occurred over time.

Note: Many of the death toll numbers are best estimates based on available research. Some, such as the Plague of Justinian and swine flu, are subject to debate based on new evidence.

Comparison of pandemics

Name	Time period	Type / Pre-human host	Death toll
Antonine Plague	165-180	Believed to be either smallpox or measles	5M
Japanese smallpox	735-737	Variola major virus	1M
Plague of Justinian	541-542	Yersinia pestis bacteria / Rats, fleas	30-50M
Black Death	1347-1351	Yersinia pestis bacteria / Rats, fleas	200M
New World Smallpox Outbreak	1520 – onwards	Variola major virus	56M
Great Plague of London	1665	Yersinia pestis bacteria / Rats, fleas	100,000
Italian plague	1629-1631	Yersinia pestis bacteria / Rats, fleas	1M
Cholera Pandemics 1-6	1817-1923	V. cholerae bacteria	1M+
Third Plague	1885	Yersinia pestis bacteria / Rats, fleas	12M (China and India)
Yellow Fever	Late 1800s	Virus / Mosquitoes	100,000-150,000 (U.S.)
Russian Flu	1889-1890	Believed to be H2N2 (avian origin)	1M
Spanish Flu	1918-1919	H1N1 virus / Pigs	40-50M
Asian Flu	1957-1958	H2N2 virus	1.1M
Hong Kong Flu	1968-1970	H3N2 virus	1M
HIV/AIDS	1981-present	Virus / Chimpanzees	25-35M
Swine Flu	2009-2010	H1N1 virus / Pigs	200,000
SARS	2002-2003	Coronavirus / Bats, civets	770
Ebola	2014-2016	Ebolavirus / Wild animals	11,000
MERS	2015-Present	Coronavirus / Bats, camels	850
COVID-19	2019-Present	Coronavirus / Unknown (possibly pangolins)	319,200*

* Johns Hopkins University estimate as of May 19, 2020
(source: https://www.visualcapitalist.com/history-of-pandemics-deadliest/)

Some older Canadians are comparing the present crisis to their memories of wartime. For comparison, below are the death statistics for the two World Wars:

Estimates of war deaths

War	Total deaths
World War I	14 million
World War II	60 million

(source: globalresearch.ca)

Shell craters, Battle of the Cambrai, France, 1918 (courtesy Ivy Images)

For others, today's situation evokes memories of the Great Ice Storm of 1998, when large areas of northeastern North America were without electricity for up to three months.

Army removing downed power lines, Saint-Jean, Que., 1998 (photo by author)

No respecter of persons

COVID-19 has already shown that no one is immune to its relentless advance — even the high and the mighty and the famous. Among the well-known figures to have tested positive for the virus are actor Tom Hanks, CNN anchor Chris Cuomo, Prince Charles, Sophie Grégoire Trudeau, U.K. Prime Minister Boris Johnson and Prince Albert of Monaco. In addition, climate activist Greta Thunberg believes that she had a light case of COVID-19 although she did not qualify for testing.

Did it need to be so serious?

An article in the medical journal The Lancet raises issues concerning the spread of the virus. An excerpt from the article follows:

> The difficulty in sifting fact from inaccurate information is aggravated by the speed of unfolding events, how much is still to be researched and understood by scientists and clinicians about COVID-19, alongside earlier deliberate obfuscation by some governments.

> Had China allowed physician Li Wenliang and his brave Wuhan colleagues to convey their suspicions regarding a new form of infectious pneumonia to colleagues, social media, and journalists without risking sanction, and had local officials not for weeks released false epidemic information to the world, we might not now be facing a pandemic.

> Had Japanese officials allowed full disclosure of their quarantine and testing procedures aboard the marooned Diamond Princess cruise ship, crucial attention might have helped prevent spread aboard the ship and concern in other countries regarding home return of potentially infectious passengers.

Had Shincheonji Church and its supporters within the South Korean Government not refused to provide the names and contact information on its members and blocked journalists' efforts to decipher spread of the virus in its ranks, lives in that country might have been spared infection, illness, and death.

Had Iran's deputy health minister, Iraj Harirchi, and members of the country's ruling council not tried to convince the nation that the COVID-19 situation was "almost stabilised," even as Harirchi visibly suffered from the disease while on camera, the Middle East might not now find itself in grave danger from the spread of the disease, with Saudi Arabia suspending visas for pilgrims seeking to visit Mecca and Medina. Neither Iran nor Saudi Arabia has free and open journalism, and both nations seek to control narratives through social media censorship, imprisonment, or even execution.

And had the Trump administration not declared criticism of its slow response to the encroaching epidemic a "hoax," claiming it was a political attack from the left, the US CDC might have been pressured to do widespread testing in early February, discovering pockets of community transmission before they dispersed widely. ("COVID-19: the medium is the message" by Laurie Garrett, The Lancet, March 11, 2020. Used with permission.)

Succeeding chapters describe the enormous impacts that COVID-19 is having on the following key aspects of our society and how people are coping with the changes and challenges being faced:

- Personal relationships
- Work and workplace
- Schooling and education
- Shopping
- Religious activities
- Travel and transportation
- Sports and recreation
- Culture and entertainment
- Finances and economy
- Research and manufacturing
- The environment
- Healthcare and hospitals
- Politics and government
- Technology
- Diversions and distractions
- Emotional response
- Silver linings

Chapter 2
Ten Commandments of social behaviour

Ten Commandments of Social Behaviour	
I	Thou shalt not kiss, hug or shake hands.
II	Thou shalt not touch thy face.
III	Thou shalt wash thy hands often for 20 seconds or more.
IV	Thou shalt cough or sneeze into thy elbow.
V	Thou shalt not gather in groups.
VI	Thou shalt not visit thy neighbour or thy relative.
VII	Thou shalt not attend special events of any kind.
VIII	Thou shalt not get closer than 2 metres to anyone.
IX	Thou shalt stay home if thou art 70 or older.
X	Thou shalt stay socially connected.

One of the most sudden impacts of COVID-19 was its effect on our social behaviour – that is, on our personal relationships. Simple things we had taken for granted all our lives were now prohibited. And we were called upon to do things differently than we had ever done them before.

Unlike the biblical Moses, who received God's Ten Commandments in one fell swoop, our code of conduct was delivered to us piecemeal as the pandemic evolved. An additional difference is that our version strikes a more positive balance between the "Thou shalt's" and the "Thou shalt not's." Below we examine each of the ten commandments in turn.

1. Thou shalt not kiss, hug or shake hands.

"I can express no kinder sign of love, than this kind kiss." – William Shakespeare

"They invented hugs to let people know you love them without saying anything." – Bill Keane

House rules cushion (photo by author)

On March 13, Dr. Theresa Tam, Canada's Chief Public Health Officer, asked Canadians to avoid kissing, hugging and shaking hands. Instead she suggested a wave or an "elbow bump" as a way of greeting someone. How unromantic these alternatives are!

For me, and I suspect for many, this commandment has turned out to be one of the more difficult to follow. I come from a loving "kissy/huggy" family and I live in a province where the two-cheeked kiss is an enshrined Quebec value. It's part of our DNA.

Bill Brownstein of the Montreal Gazette muses about the long-term result of this rule:

> Many of us – but, regrettably, not all – have become rather adept at following basic hygiene rules in seeking to ward off the coronavirus. So much so that it's hard to imagine we'll ever be able to return to our touchy-feely ways when – if? – our leaders give us the all-clear to resume our social lives. (Montreal Gazette, April 1, 2020)

2. Thou shalt not touch thy face.

This is a particularly tough order to follow because we so often unconsciously do it – whether to scratch an itchy nose, lick an index finger to turn a page, rub sleepy-seeds from the eyes or extract a wayward whisker that the razor missed. The reason that adherence to this commandment is so important is explained in this National Center for Biotechnology Information (NCBI) article excerpt:

A substantial portion of human respiratory tract infection is thought to be transmitted via contaminated hand contact with the mouth, eyes, and/or nostrils. Thus, a key risk factor for infection transmission should be the rate of hand contact with these areas termed target facial membranes. A study was conducted in which 10 subjects were each videotaped for 3 hours while performing office-type work in isolation from other persons. The number of contacts to the eyes, nostrils, and lips was scored during subsequent viewing of the tapes. The average total contacts per subject per hour was 15.7 (National Center for Biotechnology Information, June 2008)

The wearing of contact lenses is possibly a risk factor as well. Although there is not universal agreement on the subject, some experts from the American Academy of Ophthalmology suggest that wearing glasses instead of contact lenses during the current crisis may lower the chances of contracting the virus. The reasons are two-fold: a) less frequent touching of the eyes, and b) the physical barrier that spectacles provide.

3. Thou shalt wash thy hands often for 20 seconds or more.

This should be an easy one because washing one's hands is nothing more than common sense, isn't it? Yes, maybe it is, but there's much more to it. It's not as simple as putting on a pair socks – it's more like tying a tie with a Windsor knot. Both the frequency and the duration of hand washing are emphasized in this directive.

The Government of Canada spells out the following hand-washing procedure in a detailed graphic chart.

1. Wet hands with warm water.
2. Apply soap.
3. For at least 20 seconds, make sure to wash palm and back of each hand, between fingers, under nails and thumbs.
4. Rinse well.
5. Dry hands well with paper towel.
6. Turn off tap using paper towel.

4. Thou shalt cough or sneeze into thy elbow.

Although this directive predates the COVID-19 pandemic, it has been included to remind us of its critical importance. It is known that the virus spreads as a result of direct contact with the respiratory droplets of an infected person through their cough or sneeze.

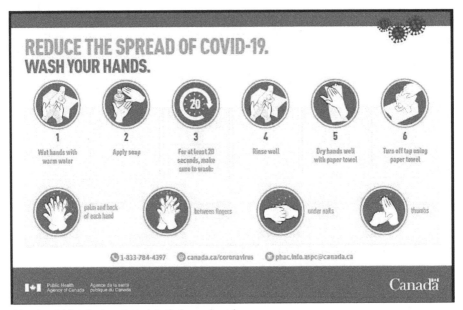

Hand washing instruction details (canada.ca)

Anatomy of a sneeze (biointeractive.org Dr. Lydia Bourouiba, MIT)

The anatomy of a sneeze is very interesting, as illustrated by the image above and the text below:

> High-speed video imaging reveals the two main components of a sneeze in colorful detail: a shower of larger droplets whose trajectories, shown in green, can extend up to 2 meters from the person sneezing (yellow),

and a cloud made of a mixture of smaller droplets suspended in moist, warm gas (red).

This second component is particularly important for estimating how far germs can spread. Direct observations, experiments and mathematical modeling show that, due to the presence and nature of this turbulent cloud, the small droplets can be carried over longer distances than previously thought, allowing them to go further than the larger drops and high enough to be sucked up into a room's ventilation system.

What does this mean? Should you feel a sneeze coming on, cover your mouth and nose with a tissue or sneeze into the crook of your elbow to disrupt the formation of the "cloud" and reduce how far your germs will spread. (https://www.biointeractive.org/classroom-resources/anatomy-sneeze)

5. Thou shalt not gather in groups.

Crowd lining up for Beatles Concert, Toronto, 1964 (photo by author)

This order came about after a rapid series of reductions in the maximum number of persons permitted to gather together. As illustrated in the table opposite, over a span of two short weeks, the limit fell from thousands to hundreds to one.

These draconian restrictions have generated

Maximum group size

Date	Jurisdiction	Limit
Feb. 29	France	5000
Mar. 12	Canada	1000
Mar. 12	Quebec	250
Mar. 21	Quebec	1

considerable debate. Section 2 of the Canadian Charter of Rights and Freedoms states that everyone has the freedom of assembly and freedom of association. But the Charter also states in Section 1 that these freedoms are "subject only to such reasonable limits prescribed by law as can be demonstrably justified in a free and democratic society." A Winnipeg Free Press article entitled "Rights and wrong in a crisis" clearly lays out this dilemma:

> The coronavirus pandemic has put civil liberties and human rights on a collision course with increasingly harsh restrictions seen around the world, to keep as many people safe and healthy as possible. Experts in this field say that, in a democracy such as Canada's, there needs to be a balance between the two pursuits and they are keeping a close eye. (Sarah Lawrynuik, Winnipeg Free Press, April 3, 2020)

Although the vast majority of Canadians have obeyed these restrictions, some have not, so authorities have had to resort to enforcement.

6. Thou shalt not visit thy neighbour or thy relative.

"Love your neighbour as yourself." (Bible, Mark 12:31, New International Version)

"Whoever does not care for his own relatives, especially his own family members, has turned against the faith and is worse than someone who does not believe in God." (Bible, 1 Timothy 5:8, New Century Version)

This directive is an extremely challenging one, especially for Christians. It is obvious that an important part of loving our neighbours and caring for our relatives is the ability to visit them.

Some neighbours essentially become part of one's extended family, and their homes and yards are treated as common property. My former Rosemere neighbours, Barb and Rick, were like second parents to our children. Not only did we exchange house keys, we were always there for each other – whether to borrow two eggs or a splitting axe; whether to celebrate a marriage or to mourn the loss of a loved one; whether to care for the children in an emergency or just to chat on the edge of our properties where our dandelion-dominated dominion met their golf-green grounds!

My daughter Andrea has experienced similar incidents of neighbourly closeness. She recounts a story about her late next-door neighbour, Marianne, whose early morning shower she interrupted to deposit her (Andrea's) young children in order to respond to a serious school emergency. In another situation, when Andrea's house was badly damaged by a burst hot water heater, her across-the-street neighbours, Marc and Korrina, welcomed her whole family into their home, where they lived for the following six months. Yes, neighbours are indeed family!

Neighbours Elaine and Dodie chat at a safe distance (photo by author)

Caring for relatives, especially the sick and the elderly, is a sacred duty that is entrusted to us. Not being able to visit them is an extremely difficult sacrifice that we are asked to endure. When this ban came into force on March 15, two of my brothers and one of my brothers-in-law were living in long-term care facilities in Quebec and Ontario. The very next day, my dear brother Malcolm (we called him "Moose") passed away following a long illness. Until that time, he had received frequent visits from his wife and his siblings. Unfortunately, my brother Jack, my brother-in-law George and so many others will be deprived of family visitors for the foreseeable future. As hard as it is, I understand the necessity of these restrictions in order to help contain the spread of the virus.

7. Thou shalt not attend special events of any kind.

First it was a restriction on attending events involving large crowds, then it was for medium-size gatherings, and finally it was a universal ban. No more sports events, rock concerts or business shows. No more yoga classes, gym workouts or spa sessions.

Not only were public events prohibited, but private ones as well. No more birthday parties, baby showers or bar-mitzvahs. No more engagement parties, weddings or wedding anniversary celebrations. No more coffee klatches, bridge games or supper club evenings.

Piper entertains at family reunion, Cookshire, Que. (photo by author)

The lack of such social events is having an impact on everyone, but especially on the seniors of our communities. Ironically, these restrictions are applied to protect that very same group of citizens who are most vulnerable to contracting COVID-19. I think of the various community outreach services such as the St. James Rosemere Drop-in Centre that my late wife Becky founded ten years ago, and which dedicated volunteers have continued ever since. Until this pandemic halted its operations in mid-March, the seniors of the area came together every Wednesday to share food, fun and fellowship. Everyone looked forward to attending because, for many, it was their only outing of the week.

8. Thou shalt not get closer than 2 metres to anyone.

Initially referred to as "social distancing," the nomenclature applied to this restriction was later modified by the World Health Organization (WHO) to "physical distancing." At its daily briefing on March 20, it said that while maintaining a physical distance was "absolutely essential" amid the global pandemic, "it does not mean that socially we have to disconnect from our loved ones, from our family."

Simply put, persons are requested to maintain a distance of at least 2 m (6 ft.) between themselves and other persons. Exceptions are made for persons living in the same household as well as in some specific work situations.

Physical distancing demonstration with two yardsticks (photo by Cameron Fraser)

Walking with physical distancing (photo by author)

Although authorities say that this rule has been followed by the vast majority of Canadians, there is serious concern about cases where some individuals have flouted it, particularly in Toronto and Vancouver. As a result, what had initially been only a recommendation became a mandatory requirement under the Quarantine Act, enforceable with heavy fines for non-compliance. CBC reported that on April 4, a New Brunswick man was handed a ticket for $292 for driving with a friend he wasn't living with. And during the week leading up to Easter, Quebec provincial police handed out almost 500 tickets to people not abiding by physical distancing measures.

On April 2, Prime Minister Trudeau said too many Canadians were still going out needlessly, potentially spreading the coronavirus and putting health-care workers at unnecessary risk. But he continued to resist invoking the Emergencies Act to issue a mandatory national stay-home order, preferring instead to count on restrictions that the provinces had already implemented.

9. Thou shalt stay home if thou art 70 or older.

Or, in the words of the oft repeated mantras: "Stay home. Stay safe." and "Stay home. Save lives."

For oldsters like me (I'm 76), this is the commandment that has impacted me personally the most. On March 14, Quebec Premier François Legault asked all Quebecers over the age of 70 to self-isolate at home. That seemed straightforward enough at first. I would simply stay put at my daughter Andrea and family's home in Saint-Lazare (Quebec), about an hour west of Montreal, where I have been living for the past two and a half years. However, I soon realized that there was a complication.

Two days earlier, on March 12, Andrea and her husband had left on a long-planned 10-day vacation to Costa Rica. Mere hours after their plane took off from Dorval airport, the Canadian government announced that, effective immediately, anyone returning to Canada from another country would be subject to a mandatory 14-day quarantine upon their return.

Embroidered wall decoration (photo by author)

This posed a serious dilemma for me, because I could not self-isolate in the same home with persons under quarantine. Either my daughter and her husband would have to pass their quarantine period somewhere else or I would have to move elsewhere to continue my self-isolation. The latter option was chosen. After considering several options as to **where** I should go, it was decided that I would move in with my second daughter, Elaine, and her family in Dorval. So I packed up my pillow, my pills and my peppermints and headed to her place. It turned out to be a very good decision because I was treated both like a privileged king (beautiful room, delicious food and lots of entertainment) and like a coddled canine (I was walked, I was groomed and I was pampered). From day one, I settled into the daily routine summarized below:

My daily routine

Time	Activity
7:00	Wake-up, shave, bath, Parkinson's pills
8:00	Old-age pills, breakfast of juice, toast and applesauce
9:00	Check emails
10:00	Morning walk with Elaine on the Lakeshore (rain or shine)
11:00	Watch Prime Minister Trudeau's daily COVID-19 update
11:30	Parkinson's pills, soup lunch and Pirate PB cookies
12:00	Watch Canadian Cabinet ministers' press conference
13:00	Watch Premier Legault's COVID-19 update
14:00	Watch other leaders' COVID-19 updates
15:00	Afternoon nap
16:00	Check emails, work on book projects
19:00	Parkinson's pills, home-cooked dinner, Pirate PB cookies
20:00	Scrabble tournament and dessert
22:00	Bedtime

10. Thou shalt stay socially connected.

At first glance, this commandment would seem to be in direct contradiction to the previous five. One might well question how it is possible to stay socially connected given the stringent straitjacket in which we have been suited. Well, let me count the ways – both online and offline.

- Email is a prime method of communicating information between computers and between people.
- Texting is a mode of communication where messages can be exchanged almost instantly between the sender and the recipient.

- Social networking services such as Facebook, Twitter and Instagram enable users to socially connect.
- Videoconferencing tools such as Zoom, Skype and Ring Central allow users in different locations to hold face-to-face meetings.
- Video sharing services such as YouTube can be used to build community. The video service can be accessed on PCs, laptops, tablets and mobile phones.
- Remember that remarkable invention by a certain Alexander Graham Bell in 1876? Ah, yes, the telephone – a device that has enabled social connectedness for 145 years and is still going strong.
- There is another venerable service that was established 100 years before Bell's invention. I am referring to what we oldies used to know as the postal service before it got remonikered by the younger generation as "snail mail." Sure, it's a bit slower than email but so much more personal. Whether it be a beautiful greeting card or a simple handwritten note, it is a wonderful way to stay connected.

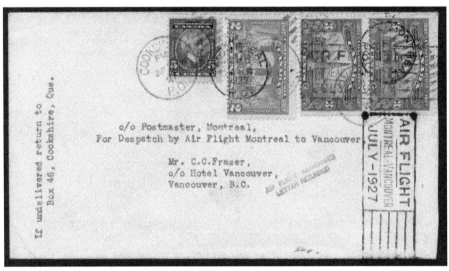

Vintage postal cover, 1927 (photo by author)

Finally, there are ways to stay connected that don't involve any device or service whatsoever. For example, doing a good deed for your neighbor, such as picking up meds or groceries, cleaning their pathway, or having a chat across the fence – all the while keeping your distance, of course!

Chapter 3
Class dismissed . . . and don't come back!

Teacher's desk on March 13 and several weeks later (photo by Sue Hartke, retouched by Greg Beck)

The Quebec government's announcement of the province-wide closure of all schools, colleges and universities on March 12 was the first indication that all was not well in the land of the fleur-de-lys. Other provinces followed suit in short order, confirming that the malaise was malignant, widespread and worsening rapidly.

Although I have never worked in the education sector, this development did affect me because I have education in my blood – it is part of the Fraser DNA. Four of my sisters were schoolteachers and currently my three daughters all work in education. That being said, I must confess that personally I hated school and would have been absolutely overjoyed had school been closed indefinitely in my day!

Public elementary and high school

The impacts of the school closures were immediate and far-reaching. Suddenly parents became home-school teachers, daycare operators and activity coordinators – often in addition to their normal day jobs.

Prior to the pandemic, parents were unsure how to facilitate their children's education at home using technology; there is little guidance on which digital tools are best, and learning online is rife with misinformation. In our new reality, parents need guidance on how to identify effective digital learning tools and strategies for their stay-at-home children. (Adam Dubé, Assistant Professor, Department of Educational and Counselling Psychology, McGill University)

Similarly, teachers found themselves in limbo as they awaited instructions from their principals, their school board and ultimately the government Education Department. Over the ensuing weeks, a sometimes confusing series of recommendations, directives and decrees were issued. Among the directives were instructions for teachers to "engage" with their students, without teaching or evaluating them. A decree was also issued that gave the government the ability to redeploy teachers to the special emergency daycares that were set up for children whose parents were working in essential jobs. Some weeks later, a second decree was issued that allowed the government to reassign education sector workers to the health care sector.

School principals found themselves suddenly becoming the chief liaison between the government/school board on the one hand and the teachers/parents on the other. My daughter Elaine, herself an elementary school principal, describes the situation:

Work seemed to continue "as usual" in some ways. Order and prepare next year's students agenda, prepare the school calendar, design and order t-shirts for next year's students, review code of conduct for printing in agenda, prepare subjects, schedules and staffing for 2020-21 as per requests from head office, etc. Many times I felt unsettled and thought, how odd to do such normal things, as life truly isn't normal right now. (Elaine Fraser)

Teacher view

As a high school teacher in Manchester, N.H., our son Liam had to suddenly shift to online learning. This was a major challenge because he works in an underserved school system where many of the students do not have access to laptops, Internet or good learning environments at home. Hazel, their very fat cat, makes a regular appearance during his daily lectures. (Pat Tracy-Callahan)

Private schools

Private day schools faced similar situations. Private boarding schools such as Stanstead College encountered an additional set of challenges. Joanne Carruthers, Acting Head of School, explains:

Stanstead College and its coat of arms, Stanstead, Que. (photos by author)

As the Acting Head during our Head's sabbatical for the 2019-2020 academic year, I could not have anticipated the challenges that our school was about to face. We were just sending students off on their two-week March break on March 12, after having meeting upon meeting to plan for the new protocols that would have to be put into place on their return, when the new decree came from the provincial government that all schools would be closed for two weeks. Carefully crafted communications had already been going out to parents and families since late January, outlining the school's response and preparations to deal with the impending crisis. Another communication went out on March 13, detailing the new procedure, which was that after the two-week break, students coming from abroad would need to spend 14 days in self-quarantine before returning to campus.

On campus, we were preparing supplies and new procedures for our health centre as well as more hand-washing stations and sanitizers campus-wide. This was in addition to the WHO hygiene and handwashing posters that had already been put up in late January, as well as hand-washing reminders at our daily family-style lunches since the start of the new year. Just a few days later, on March 16, I called in our leadership team again to further detail our plans when the federal government announced flight restrictions and anticipated border closures. At that point we began to plan for our school, like many others, to go online and begin distance education after our March break. Though we had the infrastructure and programs at the ready, and had faculty who were knowledgeable, this was nonetheless an enormous undertaking for a school that prides itself on the classroom experience. International students we had previously required to remain in Canada or the U.S. for their March break so as not to expose themselves to countries where outbreaks were still out of control, like China, Korea, Italy and Iran, were now encouraged to return home before flights became limited.

During the week of March 16 we prepared to have all our administrative staff begin to work remotely, which was also not without its challenges. By the end of that same week, we began to limit the housekeeping staff, maintenance and security personnel so that the campus buildings had essential staff only. What was always a bustling, busy, full campus, was now empty for an undetermined period of time. And jobs were on the line for those employees whose work could not be done at home. Meanwhile, our IT director and academic director began working extremely long days to prepare to train and ready our faculty to go fully online. How does a school that is so centered on the "experience in and out of the classroom" successfully move online? Time will tell as we try to not only teach online, but create an environment that keeps students engaged and ensures that we are following up with them all to hold them to task.

Our son, Tyler, is just beginning his online learning, which he is nervous about. He is a student who engages in the classroom and loves experiential learning. The move to distance education is fraught with unknowns, and he represents most students from our school who are not quite sure what to expect. He is also graduating from Grade 12 this year, and is disheartened that the school is unlikely to host the annual Baccalaureate and Graduation Service on campus in June. (Joanne Carruthers)

Colleges and universities

Colleges (CEGEPs) and universities in Quebec remained closed for two weeks before reopening on March 30 with online classes only. No physical access to the campuses was permitted. Spring convocation ceremonies have been called off. Winter 2020 and Summer 2020 semesters will

Granddaughter Micayla at online CEGEP classes from home (photo by Elaine Fraser)

proceed through remote instruction. However, there will be no in-person sit-down examinations for these semesters.

Universities in Quebec were ordered closed at the same time as schools. They reopened two weeks later but with online classes only. My granddaughters Kira-Marie, a final-year student at McGill University in Montreal, and Kennedy, a graduating student at Bishop's University in Sherbrooke, and my grandson Mattias, a first-year student at McGill, describe how the pandemic has affected their semesters:

> The global pandemic has completely impacted the end of my semester at McGill. When we first went into lockdown on March 13, professors were scrambling to figure out how they would continue teaching and assessing "as planned." Obviously, nothing about the situation would allow for the semester to proceed normally, so there was a two-week period that allowed profs to alter their content and delivery of the material. Part of this meant completely eliminating projects I had been working on for weeks or making me lead a virtual seminar using Zoom, among others. Although attending classes from the comfort of my living room was relaxing, it was also bizarre and took some getting used to. I have to give credit to all of my professors for handling this transition with grace and openness. They communicated every little change to us to make sure that everyone was on the same page. The same goes for the university's administration. Everyone really came together to make sure students felt supported during these uncertain times. This has truly been a semester to remember. (Kira-Marie Lazda)

McIntyre Medical Building, McGill University, Montreal (photo by author)

Bishop's University, Sherbrooke (Lennoxville), Que. (photo by author)

When entering my final year of university, I never imagined it would end like this. As a senior, your final year is already nostalgic in itself, so having that year cut short left many graduates feeling out of sorts. Since Bishop's University is known for its close-knit community, leaving Lennoxville felt as though I was leaving a place I called home for the past four years. Switching to online classes was definitely an adjustment. The age of the professors really dictated your course load, since many of the older professors do not mix well with technology. Thankfully enough, the professors at Bishop's are there for their students and were very understanding of the different situations this pandemic left their students in. Writing my final exams from the comfort of my own home was, without question, a different experience than writing them in the gymnasium along with 200 fellow students. Although this academic year was cut short, and many events were cancelled, Convocation was postponed until August. Once the news was released that graduation was not being cancelled, but instead postponed, many students felt a sense of relief. For us, graduation is a very special ceremony in which students are recognized for all their hard work. Although this is a bittersweet ending to my time at Bishop's, I am thankful for all the amazing people I met, the friends I made, and all the memories that come along with it. As this chapter of my life finishes, another one starts as I will be attending Concordia University in the fall to complete a graduate certificate in youth work. Hopefully by the fall of 2020 we will be able to attend school in person if everyone continues to practice social distancing. (Kennedy Fraser)

For me, not much has changed. Online classes aren't much different than regular classes. The nice thing is that you don't have to get up early anymore to make it to the 8:30 a.m. lectures since they are either prerecorded or posted afterwards. However, there is a lack of motivation that I noticed was getting larger and larger by the end of the semester. At one point, I had four lectures to catch up on which wouldn't have happened had in-person classes continued to take place. I am currently finishing up my last three exams and have barely studied for any of them due to the fear of experiencing high anxiety. Since I'm in the same room constantly, whether it's studying, sleeping, or eating, I have to be careful not to get myself too anxious. (Mattias Lazda)

In addition to the disruption of classes, the pandemic resulted in the cancellation of all university out-of-country trips and put students' summer jobs in serious jeopardy. Kira-Marie explains how it impacted her personally:

As part of my final year at McGill, I had registered to take part in a tropical ecology field course in Barbados this May. We would have been living at a research base, snorkeling every day and discovering the unique ecosystems of Barbados' coral reefs. I was really looking forward to this course because field courses offer such incredible real-world experiences and applications of the material I have been studying for the past few years. Unfortunately, COVID-19 happened and forced the school to cancel all upcoming courses requiring any sort of travel. Since this is my final semester, I will not have the opportunity to take part in the course when it is offered again next year. It has definitely been a let-down, albeit understandable given the circumstances. Regardless, I hope to go to Barbados to explore its unique ecology sometime in the future. I was also set to embark on a four-month journey doing research in Alberta's Rocky Mountains this summer. The pandemic has also placed this in jeopardy; I am currently crossing all my fingers that I will be able to go about my summer as planned, but everything is currently up in the air. The supervisor I am supposed to be doing research with said it best: "Hopefully it is a matter of 'when,' not 'if.'" (Kira-Marie Lazda)

Left: Rocky Mountains, Alberta (photo by author)
Right: Snorkelling in Barbados reefs (istockphoto.com – credit Onnes)

A friend's grandchildren faced similar difficulties:

> For three of my 14 grandchildren, who are finishing their final year at three different universities, it is extremely difficult, as they must now study and write exams online, with no libraries available for research. They no longer have friends or family around them for support, and convocations in June are postponed. Also, finding a job in the near future will be almost impossible. In addition, another grandchild, due to graduate from high school, is facing similar challenges. (Carol Alguire)

As it moved totally online because of the crisis, McGill University also enhanced its website by providing a wide range of COVID-19 related information, including the expert professional perspectives of several faculty members. Excerpts are shared in this and later chapters. (Reference: https://www.mcgill.ca/newsroom/channels/news/experts-COVID-19-309919)

Not all universities in Canada suspended teaching during the COVID-19 crisis, especially those at which online learning was already well-established. One such case was York University in Toronto, which my grandniece Lyanne attends. Her mother describes the situation there:

> York University closed their campus and moved everything online at midnight on March 13. Lyanne continued all classes and exams (even labs) online. Her work in the university fitness centre was cut off when it also closed, so her income dropped considerably. She did the last midterm of her undergraduate career that Friday, March 13, and is not sure when she will be back on campus. The university has already postponed its convocation, a huge disappointment to all the graduates. (Joanne Carruthers)

Parent views

The COVID-19 crisis meant staying at home for those family fledglings still living at home, and returning home for those living away. Affected parents share their reactions:

> Because Tyler was living in residence at Stanstead College and Lyanne was living in an apartment in Toronto, Bryan and I had been virtual "empty-nesters" since September. Having both kids now back home — and all of us living together 24/7 — has been a big adjustment for everyone. (Joanne Carruthers)

> My children are happy. My son is pleased that, no matter his score, he will pass his school year and happy that the government cancelled the final exams, while my daughter is upset that she won't be able to write those exams. What's really fascinating is that my son started an online business and manages his school tasks and business perfectly, and my

daughter set a strict daily agenda including home chores. (Lorenzo Tartamella)

I found myself trying to explain to my 4-year-old why he could no longer go to playschool (which he LOVES), why he couldn't go see his friends at daycare every Tuesday anymore, why there would be no more skating practices, and why his very first skating carnival that he had been looking forward to for months was cancelled. It was a difficult conversation for obvious reasons but also because I was trying to sort out my own emotions. (Tara Abramyk)

Words and notions like "social distancing" and "quarantine" have become our new normal. Schools here in New Brunswick are closed, as are all non-essential businesses. Grocery stores have tape on the floors with arrows directing where to walk; the number of people permitted in the store is limited. Everyone has been directed to stay home and not go out, except to get groceries or go to the pharmacy. No going to other people's homes or congregating together. If out for walks or at the grocery store, you need to keep a 2-metre distance from others. The government of New Brunswick announced that schools will not be reopening this school year. Working from home while home schooling has become the new way of doing things. Allie and Georgie will always remember Grade 3, that's for sure! (Elizabeth Harvey)

Back to school (istockphoto.com – credit delpixart)

As we are preparing to go to press at the end of April, some provinces are musing about the reopening of some schools. When that happens, the red apple on the teacher's desk will likely have been transformed into a likeness of that teacher!

Chapter 4
Whither and whether to work

Daughter Andrea's new home office in the basement (photo by Andrea Fraser)

The corona quake of mid-March dealt a stunning blow that suddenly transformed the entire Canadian workplace. Never in our history had so many profound changes occurred all at once. Previous disruptions, such as the terrorist attacks of September 2001 and the economic crisis of 2008, pale in comparison.

Fast and furious

The transformation began as a wave that within days became a tsunami. In the first of his daily addresses to the nation on March 13, Prime Minister Trudeau informed Canadians that he was self-isolating and working from home. The next day he asked federal civil servants to work from home if at all possible. Within days, several provinces had declared states of emergency, ordering all non-essential services to close. Workers were asked to stay home and to work from home wherever possible.

The fallout was immense and immediate. Some scrambled to arrange care for their children. Others moved around furniture to set up an office in their home.

Still others worried about how long the crisis would last and whether their company would survive. And everyone was concerned about the COVID-19 virus itself. Nothing was the same.

Out of work

Business CLOSED sign (istockphoto.com – credit warchi)

It happened overnight. Millions of Canadians were suddenly unemployed. No two-weeks' notice with a pink slip. You simply no longer had a job to go to. Yesterday you worked a full shift at Gaston's Garage, Tommy's Tavern, Connie's Coiffure, Suzi's Sushi or at any of the thousands of other non-essential businesses, large or small. Today you stay home and wonder when – or if – you'll be able to go back to work. And you begin to worry about how you'll be able to buy food for your family and pay the rent or the mortgage.

Work from home

An untold number of home offices were born on the weekend of March 13-15. Some of them are described here:

> I carved a workplace in the corner of our dining room – being sure to face the sun and see nature. It is necessary, more than ever, to focus on the beauty of nature amidst all the stress, sadness and uncertainty. (Elaine Fraser)

> Upon our return home from Costa Rica, Andreas and I quickly

transitioned to a routine of working from home; each of us creating our own office space in different parts of the house and purchasing equipment to try to keep our numerous meetings as "private" and non-disruptive as possible. Meeting with students and colleagues online was a bit strange at first, but it's getting easier now. Andreas's employer, MDA, brought over a load of office equipment that has now taken over the entire dining room! (Andrea Fraser)

My workplace was already at home, but because I would take frequent breaks at my local cappuccino bar, Pronto Café, now I realize how my lifestyle was truly disrupted. I came to the realization that I honestly didn't work as much as I imagined possible. Without the luxury of leaving my desk multiple times a week, I find myself actually working harder and am developing new methods on working smarter. This has been constructive and positive for me personally as I have developed and had time to test some amazingly new entrepreneurial ideas. (Lorenzo Tartamella)

Sean and I have transitioned easily into working remotely – he has the dining room table, and I am set up in the "bunk room" downstairs. We each have lots of light and views of trees and mountains. Working remotely is not new for me. I manage a group of 20+ marketing writers and graphic designers spread across New England. Some of them have been working from their homes for several years, and others move from office to office depending on workload and/or how bad the commute to Boston looked. We all have laptops, access to VPN, Microsoft Teams, Zoom, and Skype. Even if we are in our home office, chances are we're working with technical staff spread throughout the East Coast. For the past year, I have worked from home every Friday to avoid the 1.5-hour commute. Early in March, my office had started precautions, advising people to wash hands, avoid large gatherings, and travel independently to job sites and meetings. Ahead of governors' orders to stay home, our CEO had asked us to stay home; as an essential business, our offices remain open for those few who must go in.

It has been interesting to see how our technical professionals pivot to change how they work. As a large site/civil/environmental engineering firm, we are actively involved in permitting and designing major real estate and infrastructure projects. At the end of March, the Department of Transportation asked our environmental team for help adding COVID-19 requirements and revising health and safety plans for all active construction projects in the state. Over a weekend, the marketing and graphic design team met with environmental staff and our client to work out a plan to communicate the program, develop checklists, and help our client keep people working safely. We have also worked with teams to help municipalities hold virtual public meetings and conduct interviews remotely. (Pat Tracy-Callahan)

My son, who is in the final stages of getting his accounting degree, now has to do his work from home. While this means a big change in routine for us both, it is especially hard for him because he doesn't get to interact with people whom he was comfortable with. (Tracie Dougherty)

A McGill University professor describes the special challenges of working from home:

Organizations are increasingly requiring their employees to work from their homes. People who have no experience with remote work will face important challenges, such as dealing with distractions, managing the sudden overlap between their home and work responsibilities, and coordinating work projects without meeting face to face. These challenges are likely to have severe impacts on employees' productivity and mental well-being. Organizations should not push their employees into remote work and hope for the best, but instead should prepare for these upcoming issues and monitor their effects. (Jean-Nicolas Reyt, Assistant Professor, Desautels Faculty of Management, McGill University)

Essential services

For workers in jobs deemed essential (such as health care workers, public security officers and anyone involved in ensuring the grocery supply chain), it was business as usual – except that nothing was "usual" anymore.

The distinction between "essential" and "non-essential" services has been somewhat of a moving target because it varies between provinces and has also changed over time. Below is Quebec's original listing of the broad categories of essential services and commercial activities. As the pandemic evolved, different types of businesses were added to the list. For example, in mid-April, gardening stores and plant nurseries were added, effectively allowing them to reopen, albeit with special rules in place.

- Information for businesses and priority services
- Priority health services and social services
- Public security services
- Government services and other priority activities
- Maintenance and operation of strategic infrastructure
- Priority manufacturing activities
- Priority commercial enterprises
- Media and telecommunications services
- Banking, financial and other services
- Construction sector services
- Building maintenance and upkeep services
- Priority services in the field of transportation and logistics
- Work schedules and absences
- Recommendations for food establishments

It is interesting to note that the "priority commercial enterprises" category includes "Société des alcools du Québec" (liquor stores) and "Société québécoise du cannabis" (cannabis stores) but excludes Loto-Québec (lottery) terminals.

My niece Joanne reports that her husband's business was deemed an essential service: "Bryan's insurance brokerage falls under the 'essential services' heading and remains open, though the office itself is closed to the public."

My cousin Kerri's business (retail) also fell into the essential category:

> Work is so quiet – about 75% of staff working from home. I like and need the consistency of the daily routine. Our business falls under essential, so it's business as usual as much as possible. On Mondays, we arrive at work and find a sign on our desks saying that our workstations have been sanitized. I had lots of people tell me that I shouldn't be at work because my immune system was compromised. However, by Friday of the first week, my oncologist's office had assured me that I am just as able as the next person to battle the virus. I know that people were only concerned, but it was an additional stress I didn't need. (Kerri Fraser)

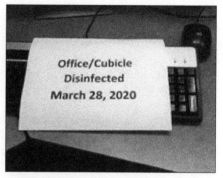

My brother David reports that his partner Nadia also works in an essential enterprise:

Sign on workstation keyboard (photo by Kerri Fraser)

Nadia Chebki at Sercovie administrative office (photo courtesy David Fraser)

Nadia works at Sercovie, Sherbrooke's "meals-on-wheels." When the isolation and distancing measures were brought out, it was very hectic. Many of the volunteers were over 70 and so had to be replaced by younger people. The cafeteria was closed. Meal delivery days were reduced and some of the hot meals were replaced with frozen dinners. However, the bigger impact for her is outside of work – waiting in line for grocery shopping, keeping her two teenaged girls occupied while limiting the time they spend on social media, and, last but not least, respecting the 2-metre distance between us, since we do not live together. (David Fraser)

Work as usual

Depending on their specific type of job, some people continued to work pretty much normally.

I work part-time (five hours per week) for United Eaton Valley Pastoral Charge as office secretary and continue to go to the office in the former Sawyerville United manse, now considered the Church. I work on my own and seldom, even during normal times, see anyone other than on my routine visits to the post office to collect the mail. The minister is currently preparing home worship services, which I edit before sending out by email, posting on Facebook and printing for those who do not have computer or Internet access. Royce and I both volunteer at the Eaton Corner Museum, Royce usually one day a week. I would normally now be organizing what needs to be done for spring cleaning as well as setting up the museum for the coming season. But, at the moment I am only checking the buildings, clearing the office answering machine and collecting the mail. (Sharon Moore Rand)

Measuring the impact

Less than a month after the crisis began, Canadians would learn the magnitude of its effect on working Canadians. On April 9, the government released the employment statistics for the month of March. The numbers were staggering. More than a million Canadians lost their jobs in March – the largest loss of jobs in a single month since record-keeping began in 1976. The unemployment rate rose to 7.8% from 5.6% a month earlier. On May 8, Statistics Canada announced that an additional two million jobs were lost in April, raising the unemployment rate to 13%.

Likewise, Canadian businesses also suffered great hardship. In the light of this dire situation, the government announced in early April a survey to better understand the challenges being faced by businesses. The Canadian Survey on Business Conditions, under the auspices of The Canadian Chamber of Commerce and Statistics Canada, sought to understand exactly what businesses were going

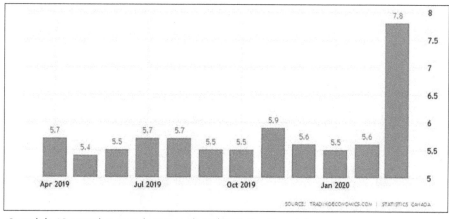

Canada's 12-month unemployment chart (Statistics Canada)

through as a result of COVID-19. Among the very detailed questions included were the following:

- Question 7: On February 1st, 2020, if this business no longer had any source of revenue, how many days could it have continued to operate?
- Question 9: Prior to February 1st, 2020, what percent of this business's workforce was teleworking or working remotely?
- Question 10: On March 31st, 2020, what percent of this business's workforce was teleworking or working remotely?
- Question 11: Of this business's workforce on February 1st, 2020, what percent is still able to carry out a majority of their duties?
- Question 12: To what extent has this business experienced the following impacts of COVID-19?
- Question 18: Compared to the period of January 1st, 2019 to March 31st, 2019, to what extent has this business's revenue changed from the same period of January 1st, 2020 to March 31st, 2020? *(Decrease in demand for products or services; Disruptions experienced by your suppliers; Unable to move or ship goods due to disrupted supply chains; Cancellation of services offered by this business; Cancellation of contracts; Uncertain accounts payable; Inability to have staff physically on-site; Staff absences due to self-quarantine; Staff absences to care for family members; Reduction in productivity due to remote work; Important meetings, gatherings or events cancelled; Travel for staff cancelled; Heightened public fear or caution causing customers to avoid this business's physical locations or services.)*
- Question 24: Which of the following new products has this business begun manufacturing in response to requests from government? (Ventilators; Masks and eye protection; Gloves; Swabs; Disinfectant

wipes; Lab testing equipment or chemicals; Gown; Hand sanitizer; Other.) (source: www.statcan.gc.ca/CSBC)

Relief programs

Bags of Canadian money (istockphoto.com – credit Shazz)

In the light of the extraordinary financial challenges faced by both employers and employees, the Canadian government has announced and implemented a series of programs to provide relief. Among them are the Canada Emergency Response Benefit and the Canada Emergency Wage Subsidy. Details of each are contained in Chapter 10. Other measures taken during the first few weeks of the pandemic to assist individuals and families included the following:

- Temporary salary top-up for low-income essential workers
- Increasing the Canada Child Benefit
- Special Goods and Services Tax credit payment
- Extra time to file income tax returns
- Mortgage payment deferral

In addition, special programs were announced to provide relief to specific groups of Canadians such as:

- Indigenous peoples
- The most needy
- Seniors
- Youth, students and recent graduates

(source: https://www.canada.ca/en/department-finance/economic-response-plan.html)

Chapter 5
Spending online vs. standing in line

Shoppers respecting physical distancing waiting to enter SAQ store in Dorval, April 2, 2020 (photo by author)

In the olden days (before online shopping was invented), shopping was like squash, spinach or sweet potato – you either liked it or you didn't. My late wife, bless her soul, absolutely adored shopping – whether to buy a cute outfit for a newborn grandchild, to purchase a different coloured sweatshirt to add to her Prismacolor collection or just to stock up on toilet paper – she loved it all. To put it plainly, she was attracted to the local mall like hornets to a strawberry jam sandwich. I was exactly the opposite and avoided shopping like the plague (I apologize for the insensitive metaphor).

Like it or not, shopping was a simple straightforward process until the dawning of the Age of Coronavirus. You went to the store, selected what you wanted, paid for it, took it home and put it away. No fuss, no bother. However, that all changed – perhaps forever – a few weeks ago, as described later in this chapter. First we will briefly summarize the various shopping models that currently exist, both online and offline.

Online shopping spike

Over the past decade, online shopping has steadily gained in popularity. Among the reasons are that it's faster, cheaper, more convenient and there is better selection. The most popular product categories have been clothing, shoes, consumer electronics, books / movies / music / games and cosmetics. According to Datareportal.com, online sales as a percentage of total retail sales has grown from 7.4% in 2015 to 13.7% in 2019. That figure will almost certainly skyrocket this year, given the current situation with so many people staying at home. And it is likely that buying groceries online will also surge in popularity.

> Canadians who have never shopped online are now joining the fray. On March 31, Numerator Canada reported that almost 1 in 10 Canadians made their first online purchase since the beginning of the COVID-19 crisis and that about 4 in 10 made their first "order and collect" purchase. (https://www.numerator.com/resources/blog/impact-coronavirus-COVID-19-canadian-consumer-behaviour)

IGA online ordering screen (www.iga.net)

A sample UPC

Bricks-and-mortar shopping transformation

Traditional stores have seen many changes over the past several decades. Probably the most revolutionary change was the introduction of the Universal Product Code (UPC) and laser scanners in supermarkets and retail stores in the early 1970s.

Much more recently, some stores have introduced "self-checkout" and "scan and go." Self-checkout machines provide a way for customers to register their own purchases before paying at a cashier pay station. Scan and go, on the other hand, requires customers to pick up a portable scanner

Bricks-and-mortar stores, Montreal, Que. (photo by author)

in the store and use it to scan the barcode on their items before putting them in their shopping basket or cart. The scanner calculates the bill and customers pay at the cashier. Both processes are alternatives to the traditional cashier-staffed checkout. Although neither of these systems has been universally embraced by consumers, it remains to be seen what effect COVID-19 will have on their acceptance and popularity.

Grocery "scan and go" (courtesy Larry Diamond)

With respect to traditional in-store shopping, many stores have made changes that aim to increase the safety of both their employees and their customers. For example, they have installed:

- Plexiglas partitions to separate the customer from the cashier
- handwashing stations for use prior to shopping
- directional floor signs to assist physical distancing

Hybrid shopping processes

There are a number of variations that combine different aspects of the shopping procedure:

- Order and collect allows the shopper to order online and collect from the store at their convenience.
- Home delivery allows the shopper to shop in-store and have the order delivered to their home.
- Phone order with delivery. For me, this is a case of Yogi Berra's "déjà vu all over again." It takes me back to my childhood in the 1950s when my parents did all their grocery shopping this way. One of my siblings or I would be delegated to telephone S.J. Osgood & Sons to place the weekly order for everything from fly-catchers to baking powder. Within an hour, the store's delivery van would appear in front of the house.

Hoarding, rationing and cherry-picking

The COVID-19 crisis has given new meaning to these time-tested practices. The hoarding of toilet paper had its origins in early March when authorities recommended that people "stock up" on essential supplies because they may have to be confined to their homes for an extended period of time. Quite logical, right? Of course! Who'd want to run out of their favourite two-ply TP when nature calls? And what about Purell hand sanitizer, the product that disappeared on day 1 of the pandemic pandemonium – probably because it, more than anything else, would protect you from the virus. Rationing, which most of us have never experienced, was the offspring of hoarding. Finally, a word about cherry-picking. Cherry-pickers, of course, are shoppers who visit a store and only buy the items that are being sold at big discounts (i.e., the weekly specials). Today, such a frugal practice is nigh impossible – unless you're prepared to stand in four different lines and have your hands washed four times in order to save a few bucks!

Hoarding toilet paper (istockphoto.com – credit RealPeopleGroup)

Shop talk

Friends and family share their shopping experiences in the COVID-19 age:

Cleaning all groceries – fruits, vegetables, canned goods, bread bags, boxes of cereal – seems so weird and it's hard to comprehend that it is such an important task. I wonder if we will always wash groceries, once this time has passed. (Elaine Fraser)

Last week when I went to the No Frills store in Brighton (Ontario) at 8 a.m., I stood in a 30-shopper queue outside the grocery store for more than half an hour. Throughout this time, a mixture of rain and snow accompanied by high winds battered and drenched us all, but I didn't hear a single soul complain. (Warren Fraser)

Shopping is limited to supermarkets or stores that have a significant food component. Up to now, we've been limiting our forays for food to once a week, usually going to two stores for milk and vegetables. We already had a well-stocked meat selection in the freezer in the basement. The stores usually have a line-up but not too long – maybe a 5-minute wait in line – and then we each go in separately in order to shop twice as quickly, with each of us having a particular list of items to purchase. (David and Margaret Gussow)

Washed groceries drying in drainer rack (photo by Pat Beck)

During the past month we have been to the grocery store twice, wine store once and pharmacy once. We have become very creative at making food from what's at the back of the freezer – some successes and a few epic fails. At least twice a week we support our favorite local restaurants by ordering takeout. (Pat Tracy-Callahan)

Recently we were encouraged to shop for our groceries online – Provigo would receive the order and prepare the order for pickup. It sounds simple. However, for us it was anything but. Several failed attempts resulted in nothing but raised blood pressures for both of us. How wonderful it would have been just to telephone Henrietta at Osgood's store like we did back on the farm and have the order delivered with no fuss! (Marilyn Reed)

We buy as much as we can at the local dépanneur in order to help him get through the pandemic. Whatever he can't provide, we buy from the grocery store in the neighbouring town of Yamaska. Since we are both over 70, it is best that we not travel there, so we order by telephone. When our order is ready, the Town arranges for it to be delivered to our door. For our medications, we had our files transferred from Drummondville to Pierreville so that they could also be delivered to our door. For hardware, we call on a neighbour. (Jacques Crépeau and Ginette Arcand)

Groceries have transitioned to being ordered online. I am still getting used to it. Seeing as you can't manage your order after you have placed it, you have to wait until the next order before you can get any ingredients that were missing. (Mattias Lazda)

This aspect has changed significantly in our household. Our prescription needs are done online at the pharmacy in Lennoxville, which in turn recommended that we have them delivered to our home. We do our grocery shopping now only every two weeks. It was a bit of a learning curve to make a list for two weeks rather than the usual once a week. We have been trying to arrive no later than 8:30 a.m., which is working well. I wear my yellow household cleaning gloves from the time my hands and the shopping cart have been sanitized until the groceries are in the trunk of the car. The gloves are put in the bags with the groceries to be worn once again at home where a sink full of warm soapy water awaits. Fresh produce is given a good rinse and left to dry. Canned or boxed goods are thoroughly wiped off. Yes, it does take longer than what was the normal grocery shopping procedure but it gives a good feeling of security. (Sharon Moore Rand)

When I go shopping for groceries, I don my oil-change black rubber gloves and wear my handyman's sawdust mask. (Charles W.K. Fraser)

Our Metro store has 7-8 a.m. shopping for seniors, which I take advantage of. The store limits the number of customers it lets in at a time and, like the nearby Shoppers Drug Mart, has floor markings to ensure the required physical distancing. (Steve Fraser)

While doing my groceries, I saw a guy at Maxi who was dressed in a long raincoat and rubber gloves that were taped to his sleeves with duct tape (just like when we used to chase bees out of the soffit when I was a teenager) and he was wearing a full-face welding helmet! (Charles C. Fraser)

Why has there been a shortage of toilet paper? A crisis created either by hoarding or artificially limiting production in a province that produces multiple paper products. And what about the shortage of eggs experienced on three separate grocery runs? Are hens now required to self-isolate and keep 2 m apart? What else are chickens expected to do but lay eggs? Flour for baking has also been in short supply in a wheat-exporting country like Canada; it's a mystery. (Lisa Taubensee)

My grocery shopping has been cut back to once a week, and that is during seniors' hours, from 7-8 a.m. or 8-9 a.m. My gluten-free baking must be ordered in advance, with a set time for pickup. When I signal my arrival, the owner brings a bag out of the store and leaves it on a table for me to collect. No human contact anymore, or chatting about life! (Carol Alguire)

Sunday grocery shopping

On March 31 Quebec Premier Legault announced that, beginning immediately, grocery stores in Quebec would be closed on Sundays in order to give grocery workers a well-deserved break. Although the government's motivation was clear, one couldn't help but see a certain irony in the situation. From the early 1900s until 1985 when it was struck down by the Supreme Court, "The Lord's Day Act" had prohibited Sunday shopping of all types, including grocery stores. During the 1990s, Sunday shopping became commonplace across the country, including in Quebec. On March 28, 2019, the Legault government introduced its Secularism Law declaring Quebec a secular society. Almost exactly one year later, the government issued the directive that closed grocery stores on Sundays.

Chapter 6
Until we meet again

Church service at St. James Church, Rosemere, Que., ca. 1980 (photo by author)

Faith communities have been dramatically impacted by the COVID-19 crisis. The ban on public gatherings has effectively denied them the ability to meet together to practice their faith. Furthermore, since many of their buildings serve as hubs for community activities, their closure impacts an even greater segment of the population. So, for the time being and the immediate future, houses of worship in Canada and around the world remain empty and quiet. Even the normally crowded St. Peter's Square in Rome is vacant. Major international and world faith gatherings have also been cancelled or postponed. The 2020 Lambeth Conference, the major gathering of bishops from across the worldwide Anglican Communion that takes place once every decade, has been postponed to 2021. And, for the first time in a thousand years, the annual Hajj pilgrimage to Mecca is expected to be cancelled.

Meeting together is important for all faiths and especially so for Christians. The Bible strongly encourages it:

Easter Sunday crowd in Saint Peter's Square, Rome 2011 (istockphoto.com – credit titoslack)

Muslims at prayer in Mecca 2014 (istockphoto.com – credit zurijeta)

> And let us consider how we may spur one another on toward love and good deeds, not giving up meeting together, as some are in the habit of doing, but encouraging one another – and all the more as you see the Day approaching. (Bible, Hebrews 10:24-25, New International Version)

The closing of churches, synagogues, mosques, temples and other religious meeting places on such a broad scale is unprecedented in Canada. Extreme weather – such as this winter's mega blizzard in Newfoundland or the Great Ice Storm of 1998 in Quebec and Ontario – may have caused the cancellation of a few services, but nothing even remotely resembling the current situation.

Muslims are also very affected by COVID-19 because their holy month of Ramadan, which begins on April 24, occurs during the midst of the crisis.

Support in times of crisis

Especially in times of major crisis, people look to their worship locations to meet together for solace and support. For example, on September 11, 2001, my own parish church held a special service that very evening to help people deal with the disaster. Churches around the world recorded increased attendance in the weeks that followed, as indicated below:

> Not since Christmas Eve had Rev. Ann Tyndall seen crowds like those who came to the Unitarian Church of Evanston the Sunday after Sept. 11. "On a normal Sunday, we would have 200 to 300 people, but we had more than 500 that day," said Tyndall. (Source: https://www.chicagotribune.com/news/ct-xpm-2002-09-06-0209060130-story.html)

> Churches were packed over the festive season as record numbers of people flocked to Christmas services . . . Church leaders believe the increase in attendance is due to a sense of unease since the September 11 attacks on New York, and that people are turning to the church for support. (Source: https://www.gazetteandherald.co.uk/news/7362127.crowds-flock-to-churches/)

A wise decision

As inconvenient as it has been for faith communities, the ban on religious gatherings was the right decision. One only has to look at what happened in South Korea much earlier in the pandemic when members of a church continued to meet even after presence of the virus was known, causing many to become infected. Or the California church that defied the state's public health stay-at-home order by continuing to hold services with parishioners, citing the First Amendment. As the old proverb advises, "Better safe than sorry."

A virtual alternative

Thanks to technology, there are alternatives (admittedly less than ideal) to meeting together in person. As soon as the ban was imposed, my tech-savvy local Anglican priest, Rev. Sophie Rolland, devised ways that members of our parish could meet virtually for services and other meetings. Among the online tools she has used are Zoom, YouTube and Facebook. She also conducted an online family funeral service for my late brother Malcolm, bringing together my 11 siblings' families from across Canada. Personally, I was very touched by the service and was struck by the timeliness of the selected scripture reading from the Book of Ecclesiastes: "There is a time for everything . . . a time to embrace and a time to refrain from embracing . . ."

Personal experiences

Family and friends share how the pandemic has affected their religious lives:

I am grateful for my faith and spiritual life throughout the uncertainties caused by this pandemic. My church family has always been important, but now, interaction through personal contacts, and on Sundays with a live-streamed service, recorded in our sanctuary (with only five people conducting the service in an empty church), is so inspiring and sustaining. Our prayers and loving concern for one another are vitally important. (Carol Alguire)

This is a test of our mental health strategies. We are required to apply what we thought we believed. It has tested the foundation of our faith. For my mental and spiritual health, I have chosen to exercise regularly by going for walks, biking along the quiet roads, stretching, and using the elliptical machine we bought second-hand just before isolation began. (Jennifer Tracy)

On March 14, together with about 100 others, I attended a funeral service in Saint-David Church. There was no handshaking and people kept their distance. Out of precaution, the priest opted for a celebration of the Word instead of the traditional funeral mass. Following the service, the people left for their homes. There was no reception in the community centre. This was the last church service that has been held there. No more choir practices and no more Sunday services. During the pandemic, Ginette and I ring the church bells for 10 minutes every Sunday at noon. The church belfry contains three bells – a large one weighing 818 kg, a medium one of 547 kg and a small one that weighs 369 kg. Astonishingly, the smallest bell bears the inscription DEFUNCTOS PLORO ("I grieve the departed") and PESTEM FUGO ("I drive out the plague"). Today the latter could be translated by "I drive out the pandemic." (Jacques Crépeau)

Couple rings church bells at noon during COVID-19 (courtesy Jacques Crépeau and Ginette Arcand)

The month of Ramadan is a time to get together, to help the needy and to bring joy to others by various means. This year, because of the pandemic, I will miss the warmth of the mosque meetings and the meal gatherings to worship God in a holy place. We also miss the visits of family and friends – even our son, Ayoub, cannot come to visit us now. Also we were in the habit of going to each other's homes to share a meal after prayers at the mosque. Normally, during Ramadan, mosques stay open all night, from sundown to sunrise, with lots of activities for everyone, including the children. But not this year. However, thanks be to God, we keep our spirits up as we do activities in our homes. (Abdellah Tabarani)

Even though I usually attend the United Church in Cookshire where I am the organist, this unusual time is giving me the opportunity to take part in the on-line worship services offered by the Anglican Church, in particular, Bishop Bruce Myers. I grew up in both the Anglican Church and the United Church. As a teenager, when confirmation classes were offered, my parents gave me the choice, and I chose to be confirmed in the Anglican Church. Most of my adult life, until returning to the Townships in 1991, I attended an Anglican Church wherever I was living. Once back in Bulwer, I, along with my late husband, Ed Laberee, began attending the local Bulwer United Church. That was where I had gone as a young child and teenager, and where Ed's family had been significantly involved over the years. Royce and I are currently involved with the little Anglican church, St. Barnabas, in Milby. (Sharon Moore Rand)

Act of God?

Poor God! He gets blamed for everything bad that happens. Of course "Act of God" is a legal term that appears in all kinds of contracts and other legal documents. Black's Law Dictionary defines it as "an overwhelming, unpreventable event caused exclusively by forces of nature, such as an earthquake, flood, or tornado." The legal community is divided as to whether COVID-19 should qualify as an official "Act of God."

Be that as it may, the Internet is replete with statements asserting that God is sending a message to the world through COVID-19. Without endorsing such assertions, I do ask myself the question. I believe that God does speak to his people in different ways in the context of different situations and that he has done so throughout recorded human history. Among the possible intentions of such messages could be to encourage, inform, admonish, intervene or a host of other ways to get our attention. I leave you to think about the possibility and draw your own conclusions. In any case, I know from personal experience that God does indeed speak to people because he has spoken to me.

Others insist that the pandemic foretells the "End Times," but many recognized scholars of biblical prophecy, like Dr. Michael Brown, dispute such a contention:

> . . . what is clear to me is that we should not view the coronavirus as a prophesied, end-time plague. Instead, we should view it in the same way we have viewed many other epidemics and pandemics in world history. They are tragic reminders of the broken state of our world and of the frailty of our race. And while doing all we can to prevent and combat the spread of COVID-19, we should pray for the mercy of God. The final shaking will be far more intense than this. (reference: https://www.christianpost.com/voices/is-the-coronavirus-an-end-time-biblical-plague.html)

It's Good Friday but Easter is coming

Crucifix and empty cross (photos by author)

For Christians, Easter is the most important religious festival of the year. I find it particularly pertinent that I am writing this chapter on Easter weekend. Today, in fact, is Good Friday – the most solemn day in the Christian calendar. As I reflect on Jesus' crucifixion, I think also of those who have already died of COVID-19 and those who will succumb to the virus before the crisis comes to an end. However, on Sunday we will experience the most joyous Christian festival as we celebrate Jesus' resurrection. At the same time, we face the future with a renewed hope, praying for the end of the pandemic.

No Easter gatherings poster (courtesy Elaine Fraser)

Because Easter is traditionally a time for families and friends to celebrate together, the government launched an intensive media campaign to plead with everyone to refrain from doing so this year.

Words of encouragement

As the COVID-19 crisis intensified, Canadian and world church leaders shared messages of hope and encouragement to their flocks and to the wider world.

> We draw hope from a variety of sources: from our religious beliefs, the love of our families, the relationships with friends and the work we do . . . Likewise, hope provides courage to face the burdens we bear and the ability to look onwards toward the dawning of a new day. In spite of present sufferings, which can seem overwhelming at times, the flames of hope cannot be extinguished . . . For religious believers, this hope takes on a special and unique dimension. It assures us of the caring embrace of the Creator, a sacred relationship sustained by prayer, and which flows into our human relationships whereby we care for one another and bear each other's burden . . . As religious leaders, we wish to emphasize, especially in times like these, the power and importance of prayer. We earnestly pray for healing, for the continued efforts to relieve human suffering, and for perseverance throughout these challenging times. (A Message to Canadians from Religious Leaders in Canada in Response to the COVID-19 Pandemic, March 30, 2020)

> I'm speaking to you at what I know is an increasingly challenging time, a time of disruption in the life of our country, a disruption that has brought grief to some, financial difficulties to many, and enormous changes to the

daily lives of us all . . . Together we are tackling this disease, and I want to reassure you that if we remain united and resolute, then we will overcome it . . . And though self-isolating may at times be hard, many people of all faiths and of none are discovering that it presents an opportunity to slow down, pause and reflect in prayer or meditation. We should take comfort that while we may have more still to endure, better days will return. We will be with our friends again. We will be with our families again. We will meet again. (Queen Elizabeth II, April 5, 2020)

It is not the time of [God's] judgment, but of our judgment: a time to choose what matters and what passes away, a time to separate what is necessary from what is not . . . We find ourselves afraid and lost. Like the disciples in the Gospel, we were caught off guard by an unexpected, turbulent storm. . .The pandemic has exposed our vulnerability and uncovers those false and superfluous certainties around which we have constructed our daily schedules, our projects, our habits and priorities . . . May God's blessing come down upon you as a consoling embrace. Lord, may you bless the world, give health to our bodies and comfort our hearts. You ask us not to be afraid. Yet our faith is weak, and we are fearful. But you, Lord, will not leave us at the mercy of the storm. (Pope Francis, March 27, 2020)

Do not be anxious about anything, but in every situation, by prayer and petition, with thanksgiving, present your requests to God. And the peace of God, which transcends all understanding, will guard your hearts and your minds in Christ Jesus. (Bible, Philippians 4:6-7, New International Version, quoted by Marcelle McPhaden, President and CEO of Health Partners International of Canada, a charity dedicated to increasing access to medicine and improving health in vulnerable communities)

A pastor's point of view

A long-time friend of mine, Pastor John, reflects on what the COVID-19 crisis has meant to him, how it has affected his congregations and how it has brought new clarity to the Christian message.

Pastoring is neither a job, nor a chosen occupation, but rather a vocation, and with this vocation comes certain very specific and serious responsibilities. A pastor's charge is not only the preparation of a Sunday sermon, along with various administrative and other housekeeping tasks necessary to keep a church in good order. Being a pastor means that one is directly responsible before God for the spiritual safety, nourishment and well-being of those entrusted to him or to her. The upheaval caused by the COVID-19 crisis has done much to help us to understand more clearly and appreciate better this truth.

The church as a family, as a body or as a flock, flourishes best when it experiences life together under the protection and watchful eye of a good shepherd. As thankful as we all are for technology that enables us to conduct "virtual" on-line services and Bible studies, there is definitely something missing in any of these endeavours. That something is close, personal contact and a living, vital (not virtual) relationship one with another as a church. Not too long ago, it would have been difficult to imagine a family whose members were only connected by technology, although today such a scenario is quite feasible, and even becoming the norm in certain households. In the not too distant past, most families had at least one meal together each day, usually the evening meal, where food and fellowship were shared on a regular basis. The community aspect of church, as Christ intended it, was never, never one in which the members exist alone or in isolation. It is impossible to "do church" alone, cut off one from another. Our attempts to remain connected via the Internet and by other means are good, but still, it's just not the same. We are waiting and longing for that day when restrictions will be lifted and we can be together again, worshipping God as a family.

So, what's a pastor to do? How do we pastor a flock which can no longer come together as a body? In our case, we have followed the general trend and have reluctantly begun to broadcast our Sunday sermons via Facebook. To compound the complexity of the situation, the few members we do have in our two congregations (one French, one English) are mostly elderly and are not adept at using on-line technology. The majority of our people do not own a computer or cell phone, and so our on-line messages never reach them. In order to keep a sense of connectivity and community alive, we have done two things which seem to be effective for the moment. First of all, we have established a community prayer time, which we observe at or around 6:00 p.m. each day. A program was written, printed and delivered to each home. The packet contains a cover letter, a copy of Psalm 91 and various relevant passages of scripture and prayers. Each evening, our members recite Psalm 91 in their homes, read the passages of scripture and pray for our church, its needs and the needs of the community. Because of social distancing regulations, some have even had their daily prayer meetings via telephone with other members of the church. This idea, which seems to be working quite well, was actually proposed by a member of the church who had a deep yearning for a continued sense of community.

As pastor, we have also made it a point to maintain regular telephone contact with our members. Our calls are usually brief, a sort of check-up on how people and their families are doing. Sometimes, the call can become quite lengthy because the church member just needs to talk to someone. We read in the newspapers that loneliness and isolation are taking their toll on people's mental and emotional health, and sometimes a pastor can inadvertently become a healer simply by listening. This too seems to be effective and much appreciated.

While we rejoice in the measure of success that we have enjoyed through these temporary measures aimed at keeping our group intact and connected, I feel that most of us who are in the ministry realize that this is not a "permanent fix." To summarize, other than causing us to pray more than we ever have before, the main effect of the current COVID-19 crisis upon us in the ministry has been to significantly raise our appreciation for the communal aspect of the body of Christ. As St. Paul so succinctly stated in his first letter to the church in Corinth, "the body is one and has many members" (I Corinthians 12:12) so that none of us can say to the others "I have no need of you." (I Corinthians 12:21). The gathering together of the saints of God in worship and fellowship is not only an integral part of what it means to be the church, it is its defining characteristic and trademark. The COVID-19 pandemic has illustrated this to us in a very real and effective way. It is a privilege that we treasure more and more, as restrictions continue and we remain confined to our homes. (John Thévenot)

In closing this chapter, I share two verses of the hymn "God be with you till we meet again," composed in 1880 by a distant relative of mine, Jeremiah Rankin, that gives needed encouragement in the present circumstances:

God be with you till we meet again,
When life's perils thick confound you,
Put His arms unfailing round you,
God be with you till we meet again.

God be with you till we meet again,
Keep love's banner floating o'er you,
Smite death's threatening wave before you,
God be with you till we meet again.

Chapter 7
Travel tales and fails

Diamond Princess "Corona cruise," Toba, Japan, February 2020 (photo by Monique Marson Stever)

Travel had a dual role to play in the COVID-19 pandemic tragedy – virus travel and people travel. In this chapter we examine how the coronavirus spread from continent to continent, country to country, region to region and finally person to person. We will also look at some of the many ways that COVID-19 impacted people's travels during the crisis.

Virus on the move

As indicated in the following table, many of the first cases in the different countries were travellers returning from China. The rest were from contacts with already infected persons. COVID-19's coronaquake epicentre became a fast-moving target as it rapidly and relentlessly made its way across the world, infecting Asia, Europe and North America in the space of one month. Eventually, it infected practically every country in the world.

The spread of COVID-19

Country	Date of first case	Source of infection
China	17/11/2019	Unknown, but likely an animal source
Japan	16/01/2020	Travel from Wuhan
USA	21/01/2020	Travel (China)
Hong Kong	22/01/2020	Travel from China mainland (via rail)
France	24/01/2020	Travel from China
Canada	25/01/2020	Travel (Wuhan, China)
Germany	27/01/2020	Contact (Chinese business partner in Germany)
Italy	30/01/2020	Contact (Chinese tourists from Wuhan)
Spain	31/01/2020	Contact (infected person in Germany)

(sources: WHO and other Internet sources)

Air rescues

The rapid-fire closure of international borders in March left thousands of Canadians stranded in many areas of the world. In response to this aspect of the crisis, the Canadian government negotiated with several foreign governments to arrange safe passage flights back to Canada. Among the countries from which these rescue flights departed were

Jet coming in for a landing, Montreal, Que. (photo by author)

Morocco, Peru and India. In addition, Canada sent rescue planes to repatriate hundreds of Canadians from coronavirus-infected cruise ships in Japan and the United States.

On the rails again

After being derailed for several weeks by the First Nations blockades in support of Wet'suwet'en Hereditary Chiefs in British Columbia opposing pipeline construction, Canadian passenger rail service just got back on track when COVID-19 arrived. On March 15, Via Rail Canada announced reduced schedules, modified meal service and enhanced cleaning protocols. Two weeks later, the company informed its clientele of the following additional measures.

- A series of health checks will be conducted by VIA Rail employees with customers before boarding our trains. This will include asking simple health questions and looking for visible signs of illness prior to boarding.

- Passengers will be denied boarding our trains if:
  - They are experiencing symptoms similar to a cold or flu (fever, cough, difficulty breathing)
  - They have been denied boarding for travel in the last 14 days due to medical reasons related to COVID-19

VIA Rail passenger train, Manitoba (photo by author)

Travel tales

On March 12, Andreas and I left for a vacation in Costa Rica. At the time, although COVID was now taking hold in parts of Europe and Iran, there was very little going on in Central America. There were no travel advisories for the area, yet people were being cautious everywhere just the same. We were in a very remote part of the country that receives few tourists; the type of place we typically visit anyway, but this year it was especially helpful. During the day while we explored the jungle, we were completely immersed in the beauty and peace of nature. At night when we would go online to check what was happening back home, we felt the level of public anxiety in Quebec ramping up as increasingly stringent measures were put in place to try to contain the COVID beast. Due to the potential closure of borders, we made arrangements to come home early and begin our quarantine. At that time, it was really only me that would have had to self-isolate for two weeks because I work in the education sector. I would have been back at work on April 3; only four days after everyone else would be back on March 30. A few days later, by the time we landed in Montreal, schools were closed until May and everyone was required to self-isolate after returning to Canada from anywhere! We drove ourselves home from the airport and were greeted by only the dogs – Dad having cleared out and gone to Lainie's while we served out our quarantine. Dad got to spend some quality time with Lainie and family, and the Dorval waterfront on their daily walks. After successfully serving our quarantine, we welcomed him back home on April 3. Out of curiosity, we have kept an eye on the progress of the disease in Costa Rica and were not surprised that the numbers of active cases remained very low for a long time. In fact, there were none in the area where we spent the majority of our time. However, Costa Rica, like most other countries around the world, closed its borders to new international visitors on March 18 as well as closing access to national parks, restaurants, bars etc. at the same time. (Andrea Fraser)

In late February, my partner, Dave, and I went to St. Anton (Austria) to ski and were surprised that our friends from Munich were so sick that they had to stay home. Last week, they tested positive for COVID-19, along with a daughter and son-in-law who had stayed with them in their St. Anton apartment. While there, a German woman was too sick to have dinner with us. She too recently found out that she had the virus. There were three of us at a very small table that evening, so we could very likely have caught it. On March 9, Dave went back to Canada and I went to visit my friend, Martha Shearer, in Provence (France). On March 12, Martha flew to Canada to visit her brother in an Ottawa hospital. Realizing that I should leave also, I packed and left by train for Zurich, where I arrived early the next morning. I was able to get a seat on a Swissair flight to Montreal the next day. Meanwhile, Switzerland suddenly closed the border with Austria on March 13 because there were too many COVID-19 cases there. So I consider myself very fortunate on two counts: not having contracted the virus in Austria and being able to return to Canada when I did. (Margaret Eastwood)

Homeward bound

More than a quarter of a million Canadians go south for the winter. When the Canadian government in mid-March urged all its citizens to return home, it posed a dilemma for these snowbirds. Should they abandon the sunny south and head for home sweet home in the cold white north or stay put and "ride it out?" Two Canadian snowbirds wintering in Mexico share their return adventure stories:

We spent the winter in Ixtapa, Mexico. The weather was great and we had a very nice condo on the ocean. Then news started to arrive from all over about the coronavirus – first China, followed by Italy and Spain, and then Canada and the U.S. Even though there were no reported cases in Mexico, the Americans and Canadians began to worry about getting back home because the governments were starting to close their borders. Many people were booking early flights at any cost just to get home. One couple paid $1200 each to return to Toronto two days ahead of their prepaid booked flight!

We had three weeks to go before our scheduled flight home, but it was almost impossible to reach the airlines by phone or Internet to change our reservation. We found a flight out of Mexico City that would have taken us two full days to return. So we decided to stay, not knowing whether our scheduled Air Canada flight would actually operate. It did arrive on time. However, due to the timing, we would now have to go

Sun and sand in the south (photo by author)

into the 14-day quarantine at home upon our return. And there were other complications awaiting us at home.

Our friends had their kitchen totally gutted while we were away, so we had offered our house for them to stay in. In the meantime, the cabinet company doing their renovations had to shut down because of COVID-19. Therefore our friends would have nowhere to go because we had to be quarantined in our own house. We had another option; however, we could not go to our country house up north because by the time our quarantine was over, the police were giving tickets if people moved from one region of Quebec to another. So that was one more problem to solve. Finally our friend with her two kids moved in with us. We have been locked in our house for four weeks now. My sister Charlotte and brother Danny and friends have been bringing us food to the house. That is going well but I hope this monster will end soon. (Bob Taylor)

For at least twelve years we have gone to Ajijic, Mexico (an hour south of Guadalajara) for the winter. Last year we rented a villa – two bedrooms and two bathrooms, living room, dining room and kitchen – at Nueva Posada. It is a hotel that is gradually being turned into condos. We arrived in Mexico on January 9. All was most enjoyable – friends, dinners. Then the C-stuff arrived on TV and we booked a ticket home for April 1. However, Aero Mexico cancelled our flight from Guadalajara via Mexico City to Toronto. We booked the next flight we could get, on Interjet, a Mexican sort of Transat, leaving the next day for Toronto. As we went through security at the Guadalajara airport, two Red Cross workers in full gear and with testing equipment stopped us for a fever check. They were backed up by a couple of Federales, state police, who liked to fondle their large, and multiple, firearms. We flew overnight to Toronto. Upon arrival, we were greeted by a group of uniformed, nicely pressed pants and shirts, who said "Welcome home, have a good time and self-isolate for the next 14 days" and treated us to coffee and munchies. We took a limo to our condo at St. Clair and Yonge where the concierge sprayed our hands before they let us in. And here we stay to wait out our sentence! I think I would have been happier staying in Mexico. (Frank Hall and Linda Bergman)

At the Mexico City airport, my friend Frank met a Canadian man who shared an amazing tale about his own incredible adventures involved in returning home to Canada from Guatemala. Frank remembers the story as follows:

He had been in Guatemala City, not sure why, but all flights out of the country were cancelled, so he and some Americans pooled their funds for a taxi to the Mexican border. At that point he walked (or perhaps swam) across the border into Mexico. The Mexican military is very present there to stop illegal crossings. So, certainly it was not a safe or legal method, even though he had a Canadian passport. Then he succeeded in finding a 16-hour bus ride to Mexico City – the cheap variety where the second driver slept in a sleeping bag in the cargo hold. (I have ridden the bus system, the luxury version only, but I believe that what he said was true for the cheaper passage.) Next was the five-hour flight to Toronto, then a bus to Sudbury, and finally hitching a ride to his home. (Frank Hall)

Personal travel comments

People recount how their own personal travel has been impacted by COVID-19:

The price of gas has never been so affordable, but since we can't go anywhere, who benefits? (Lisa Taubensee)

Cheap gas (photo by Elaine Fraser)

This is a major difference for us. In 2019 we travelled out of the country for 105 days. It's down to zero for this year. Driving the car to the supermarket is the only place we are going! (David and Margaret Gussow)

We have stopped travelling outside of our own municipality, so we hardly use our car at all. No more of the frequent visits to family in Saint-Eustache, Drummondville or Beloeil — we are confined to Saint-David. The best part of it is that it is cheaper and contributes to a reduction of greenhouse gases. (Jacques Crépeau and Ginette Arcand)

COVID Cancellations

For more than a year, my brother Jim and I have been working to organize a family heritage tour of Normandy (France) in August for 20 of our extended kin. Everybody had paid their first two instalments, the itinerary was finalized and several had already booked their flights. Then COVID-19 burst our travel balloon. We have postponed the trip to the summer of 2021. Others share their COVID-caused cancellations below.

We had scheduled and paid for a Mediterranean cruise to take place April 19 to May 10, 2020. This Crystal Cruise would begin in Venice and end in Barcelona (two of our favourite European destinations). The cruise line cancelled the cruise last month and will refund 75% but keep 25% as a credit for a future cruise (which did not please me). It will be interesting to see how cruise companies will react long-term to this pandemic. In June, three of my pals and I have booked and paid for 10 days of golf around Scotland. We are now in discussions with the tour company as Canada says no pleasure travel to the U.K. And, of course, the U.K. has its own issues (as do all). (Bob Simon)

This has been a difficult time for me as it was 46 years ago that [my husband] Ed died in Bermuda. I was due to take a trip there, but it was cancelled due to the pandemic. Also, a close friend there lost her husband, and had to have a graveside interment for immediate family only. No others were allowed, so I couldn't have attended, even if I was there. Sad times. (Carol Alguire)

Commuting precautions

Physical distancing was no problem on the 202 bus that passed by my daughter's house every 20 minutes because there were rarely more than two riders and often it was completely empty. Nevertheless, all precautions were taken, including bus driver protection by forcing passengers to enter and exit by the back door only. Since the fare collection/validation station beside the driver is inaccessible, rides are essentially free.

Montreal bus rider enters via back door (source: https://www.cbc.ca/news/canada/montreal/stm-exposure-1.5500292)

On April 16, Montreal mayor Valérie Plante announced that the city would help fund protective measures for taxi drivers, such as the installation of Plexiglas barriers and purchasing of hand sanitizers. There would be subsidies of up to $190 per taxi.

Empty Dorval city bus (photo by author)

Travel restrictions

Over a period of one week, the Canadian government issued a series of travel advisories and restrictions.

- March 13: The federal government is warning against all international travel. Canada's chief public health officer asks Canadians to postpone or cancel all non-essential travel outside the country. Canada is also banning cruise ships carrying more than 500 people from docking at Canadian ports until July.
- March 16: Prime Minister Trudeau announced that Canada would be

barring the entry of all travellers, other than Canadian citizens and Canadian permanent residents.

- March 18: Prime Minister Trudeau announced that Canada and the United States had agreed to temporarily close the Canada-U.S. border to non-essential travel.

Diamond Princess "corona cruise"

On January 4, Quebecer Monique Marson Stever, an adventurous septuagenarian, boarded the Diamond Princess cruise ship for a one-month Asian cruise, but she got much more than she had bargained for. She tells her story:

Cabin for my 16-day quarantine on the ship (photo courtesy Monique Marson Stever)

The cruise itself went very well as we made stops in Hong Kong, Vietnam, Japan and Taiwan. On February 4, the last day of the cruise before our scheduled disembarkation the next morning, we packed our bags and placed them outside our cabins before our final evening dinner. But when we returned after dinner, we discovered that our luggage had been put back inside our cabins, so we knew that something was not right.

The captain informed us that cases of COVID-19 had been discovered on board. As a result, the ship was quarantined in the port of Yokohama (Japan), and I spent the next 14 days confined to my windowless inside cabin. Accepting my fate, I passed my days solving Sudokus, surfing the web and learning tai-chi. During the final four days, as the number of infection cases mounted rapidly, the ship broadcast multi-faith prayers accompanied by beautiful calming landscapes. Fortunately, at the end of the quarantine period, I showed no signs of the virus so (along with other Canadian passengers) was flown back home to Canada on February 21.

Upon arrival at CFB Trenton, we were immediately placed in a second 14-day quarantine at the NAV Centre in Cornwall (Ontario).

Finally, on March 5, I returned to my hometown of Saint-Jean-sur-Richelieu (south of Montreal) where I resumed my normal routine. But alas, my "freedom" was short-lived. On April 2, like other Quebec seniors, I entered indefinite self-isolation – my third quarantine in just over two months. In spite of it all, I have absolutely no regrets and am looking forward to taking two more cruises later this year! (Monique Marson Stever)

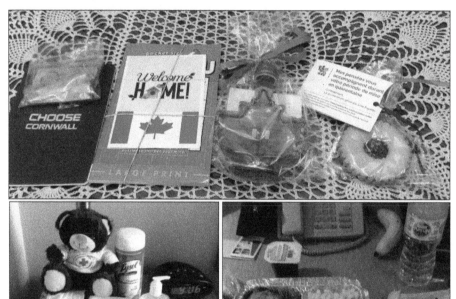

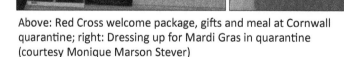

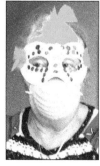

Above: Red Cross welcome package, gifts and meal at Cornwall quarantine; right: Dressing up for Mardi Gras in quarantine (courtesy Monique Marson Stever)

Unfortunately, not all passengers of the Diamond Princess had such a positive outcome. Of a total of 3,711 passengers and crew members, 712 tested positive for the virus and 10 have died.

Impact on airline industry

With all the travel restrictions in place, the airline industry has been dealt a heavy blow by the crisis.

- Air Canada laid off 16,500 workers
- WestJet announced 6,900 departures comprised of early retirements, resignations and both voluntary and involuntary leaves
- Transat AT Inc. laid off at least 3,600 flight attendants

Expert view

From a forecast of continued profitability and growth for the aviation community to a questioning of survival for many in the industry, the economic and social fallout of the COVID-19 virus continues to impact demand for air travel and the supply of aviation capacity. As airlines are reducing operations that were primarily focused on passengers, many are now looking to operate passenger aircraft to move only cargo. The need to move components in critical supply-chain scenarios will need air freight capacity, well beyond that offered by freighters. The challenge will be to ensure that commercial aviation does not reduce capacity to the point of impacting critical supply chain needs. (John Gradek, Faculty Lecturer, School of Continuing Studies, McGill University)

Chapter 8
Wait 'til next year!

Opening Ceremonies, 1976 Summer Olympic Games, Montreal (photo by author)

A variety of common sports-related terms may be invoked to describe the huge effect that COVID-19 has had on the world of sports.

- shutout (hockey)
- knockout (boxing)
- rain out, snow out (baseball)
- timeout (basketball, football, hockey)
- strikeout (baseball)
- wipeout (cycling, surfing, skiing, skating)
- lockout (various pro sports)
- the finish line (track, skiing, car racing, etc.)
- time's up! (end-of-game whistle/buzzer/siren (various sports))

"Wait 'til next year!"

But there is one expression that summarizes the current situation better than any other. Permit me to share a bit of personal history to introduce it. As a young kid, I was a rabid baseball fan – that was many long years ago – before the Montreal

Expos came and went. I was a Brooklyn Dodgers fan. I remember listening to their games on my transistor radio that devoured batteries at a rapid (and expensive!) pace, especially when I would fall asleep listening with it still turned on. For years, I faithfully followed the heroics of Jackie Robinson, Duke Snider, Pee Wee Reese, Don Drysdale, Roy Campanella and all the others. We never had a TV at home when I was growing up, so the only time that I ever saw baseball being played live was when my uncle invited us over to watch the classic Yankees-Dodgers World Series match-ups of the early 1950s.

The Dodgers were a great team and won five National League pennants between 1941 and 1953. However, try though they might, they would lose the World Series to their American League arch-rivals, the New York Yankees, all five times. As a result, the unofficial battle cry of the long-suffering Dodgers fans became "Wait 'til next year!"

Such is the current situation for a long list of sports events that have been postponed or cancelled due to COVID-19. Some may yet happen later this year but for most of them, everyone – like the Dodgers fans of yore – must wait until next year.

Fan ban

Italy soccer match with empty stadium (istockphoto.com – credit simonkr)

Among the earliest indications that COVID-19 spelled trouble for the sports world here in North America were restrictions put in place in Italy and Japan in early March. In Italy, where cases of COVID-19 were mounting rapidly, authorities announced that all sporting events through April would be conducted in empty stadiums, including Series A soccer games. And in Japan, where relatively few cases had yet been detected, the country's top baseball league was already playing its spring training games without spectators. These situations were harbingers of what was to come on this side of the pond.

Sporting events ban

It didn't take long before the sports world realized that sports without fans was a bit like apple pie without ice cream. Almost instantly, league schedules were suspended and planned events were either postponed or cancelled outright. No sport, either professional or amateur or any other, was immune from this fate. Some of them are highlighted here to indicate the breadth of the shutdown.

Pro leagues

The NBA (National Basketball League) was the first to throw in the towel, and they did it in very dramatic fashion. On March 11, a game in Oklahoma City between the Utah Jazz and the Oklahoma City Thunder was ready to get underway. Players were already on the floor for warmups and the opening tip was just moments away when the players were told to return to their locker rooms. Fans were told about 30 minutes later that the game was postponed "due to unforeseen circumstances." As it turned out, one of the Utah Jazz players had tested positive for COVID-19.

The next day the league announced that it was suspending the league schedule. That move had an immediate domino effect as, one by one, the other professional leagues made similar announcements.

On the same day, the NHL (National Hockey League) suspended its 2019-20 season. The previous night, the Montreal Canadiens had played the Nashville Predators at the Bell Centre in Montreal and my grandson Caleb was there. It was a very special occasion as homage was paid to the recently deceased former Habs star, Henri "Pocket Rocket" Richard.

Major League Soccer also suspended their season, affecting Canadian teams in Toronto, Montreal and Vancouver. The Montreal team was further impacted by suspension of the CONCACAF Champions League.

The National Basketball League of Canada put an end to its 2019-20 season.

Major League Baseball announced that its schedule would be suspended for at least eight weeks, starting March 16.

The Canadian Football League postponed the start of its regular season until the beginning of July.

Montreal Canadiens tribute to Henri Richard at final game before COVID closure (photo by Nick Derby)

Special sporting events

In addition to the suspensions or postponements of the professional league schedules, many eagerly anticipated sports championship events were also cancelled or postponed, much to the disappointment of fans and athletes alike. Some of the events listed below were only cancelled at the very last minute, as the seriousness of the COVID-19 pandemic became apparent:

- World women's hockey championship, March 31 to April 10 in Halifax and Truro, Nova Scotia, cancelled.
- World figure skating championships, March 16-22 in Montreal, cancelled.
- World women's curling championship, March 14-22 in Prince George, B.C., cancelled.
- Canadian Grand Prix in Montreal, June 12-14, postponed.

- Rogers Cup tennis tournament in Toronto and Montreal, cancelled or postponed.
- Wimbledon Grand Slam Tennis Tournament in London, England, cancelled.
- Boston Marathon, cancelled.
- North American Indigenous Games July 12-18 in Kjipuktuk (Halifax), Aldershot and Millbrook, Nova Scotia, postponed.
- Queen's Plate thoroughbred race at Woodbine Racetrack in Toronto, postponed indefinitely
- Arctic Winter Games, March 15-21 in Whitehorse, cancelled.

The Olympic Summer Games

The biggest international sports event of all – the Summer Olympic Games – could not be spared from the sword of Damocles even though it had resisted pressure from athletes for weeks. On March 23, the Tokyo Games were postponed to an undetermined date in 2021. Sometime later, the new date was announced as July 23 to August 8, 2021. Most athletes welcomed the postponement, while at the same time recognizing that it would mean delaying or even quashing the realization of their dreams. Canada's world-class racewalker, Evan Dunfee, shares what the postponement means to him:

The Olympics is something we plan our lives around. Every four years are planned out. You know where your major races are going to be each year, you have a good idea of where you'll be on any given day 3-4 years ahead of time. After winning a World Championship medal last fall, I was confident that all the work we had been doing was getting ready to pay off in Tokyo. Once it started to become clear that this pandemic was not going to allow the Olympics to safely take place this summer (and that realization came days if not weeks before the IOC actually buckled to the pressure to make any sort of decision) I thought that I'd feel lost, disappointed or empty. Instead I felt excited. I'm very fortunate – I get to compete in sport for a living. And if I have to wait one more year at another shot at my dream, that is nothing

Canadian champion racewalker Evan Dunfee in action (photo by Terry Shaw)

because right now millions of people are faced with maybe losing their dreams. Like all the restaurants, small businesses that may never open again, the high school senior missing out on their grad, or their final sports season. I'm so fortunate that my dream is only delayed and not gone. I'm also blessed in that training for my sport involves going out and wandering around for hours on end on the roads. It is something that I am still able to do by myself while avoiding contact with others. Some of my training has been adapted, like avoiding the track, and obviously, being without my strength coach and physio, things are a bit tough. However, some athletes out there have had to change their entire routines. Swimmers, for example, trying to stay fit without access to a pool. So, in so many ways, I consider myself very fortunate. I hope that I can use this extra year as well to get a little faster, a little stronger and a little closer to my goal of standing atop the podium at the Olympic Games. (Evan Dunfee)

Local sports and recreation closures

Boys Midget B hockey game, Pointe-Claire, Que. (photo by Elaine Fraser)

Perhaps the greatest impact of all involves the closure of all municipal and community sports and recreation facilities including parks, playgrounds, pools, arenas, gyms, spas and many more. My grandson Caleb's inter-city hockey season ended abruptly, just before the start of their playoffs.

For anyone taking fitness seriously, the closures represent more than an inconvenience – it is a question of health. On the other hand, for couch potatoes, life continues uninterrupted. Some of our contributors share their comments about the impact of COVID-19 on their activities:

The closing of outdoor natural areas has had a large impact on our physical conditioning. The first restrictions that impacted us directly were the progressive restrictions on activities within – then even access to – Gatineau Park. Thus, the cross-country skiing season ended

Kids on playground (photo by author)

Playgrounds closed signs. Above: Dorval (photo by author); right: Peterborough (photo by Carol Rand)

approximately one month earlier than last year. For the past several weeks we are not even permitted to walk across the bridge from Ottawa (Ontario) to Gatineau (Quebec). (Jim Fraser)

I am a huge fan of the London Knights OHL hockey team, attending games over the past few years quite regularly. This season they had a very good team (2nd in the 31-team league) and I believe had a great chance to win the Memorial Cup. But alas, that was not to be, as all junior league teams were shut down in early March. (Steve Fraser)

91

Barricaded gazebo (photo by author)

Warning sign on city park bench, Ottawa (photo by Jim Fraser)

Spreading the message

Several well-known Canadian sports personalities, including Shea Weber, Hailey Wickenheiser and Laurent Duvernay-Tardif, have been recruited to help deliver the government's COVID-19 physical distancing and stay-at-home messages to the public. Recently I received a cellphone recorded voice mail from Montreal Canadiens captain Weber exhorting me to continue to respect the restrictions.

Chapter 9
The show must NOT go on

Museum CLOSED sign, Dorval, Que., April 2, 2020

We are probably all familiar with the phrase "The show must go on." The saying originated in the 19th century with circuses. If an animal got loose or a performer was injured, the ringmaster and the band tried to keep things going so that the crowd would not panic. With the coming of COVID-19, the expression, like so many other things, has been turned on its head. Indeed, we now know that the show, whatever form it may take, must NOT go on. Whether it be music or museum, culture or agriculture, dance or drama, comedy or cabane à sucre – the doors are closed and the show will not go on.

It is interesting to note that, unlike the sporting events which were mostly all cancelled right away, many of the events listed below weren't cancelled until the last minute. Perhaps this was because optimistic organizers were hoping against hope that their event might be able to go on as planned. But, in the end, that was not to be.

Major musical events

Following is a small sampling of the hundreds of major musical events (concerts, festivals, awards ceremonies and other industry events) cancelled or postponed due to COVID-19:

(istockphoto.com – credit hatman12)

- Bon Jovi 's 2020 North American tour was cancelled.
- Shania Twain has cancelled all of her Las Vegas residency performances at the Zappos Theater.
- Justin Bieber announced the postponement of his 2020 Changes Tour.
- Garth Brooks has rescheduled his upcoming stadium concerts.
- New Orleans Jazz & Heritage Festival, scheduled to take place April 23-26 and April 30 to May 3, will now be moved to the fall.
- The Rolling Stones announced that their 15-date No Filter Tour has been postponed.
- Elton John has postponed his Farewell Yellow Brick Road tour to 2021.
- The 55th annual Academy of Country Music Awards have been postponed.
- Céline Dion postponed the March and April dates of her Courage World Tour in North America.
- Taylor Swift was scheduled to headline Capital One's JamFest in Atlanta on April 5, as part of the 2020 NCAA March Madness Music Festival. The event has been cancelled.
- Miley Cyrus cancelled her trip to Australia for the World Tour Bushfire Relief concert.

(source: https://www.billboard.com/)

Theatre

Theatres, like other entertainment venues in Canada, have been seriously affected by the COVID-19 pandemic:

- The very popular classical theater, the Stratford Festival, has cancelled all performances scheduled for April and May.
- The Shaw Festival, a major not-for-profit theatre festival in Niagara-on-the-Lake, Ontario, is the second largest repertory theatre company in North America. Its performances are cancelled until at least July.
- The Toronto Fringe Festival, an annual theatre festival, featuring un-juried plays by unknown or well-known artists, has been cancelled.

Montreal summer festivals

Montreal is widely known for its abundance of summer festivals that together attract millions of tourists and locals in a normal year. But not this year.

- On April 7, Mayor Valérie Plante announced that, among the events affected, are the Just For Laughs comedy festival, which she hoped would be rescheduled for August or September.

- Organizers of the Montreal International Jazz Festival, the Francopholies and the punk Pouzza Festival have all previously said the events would not be held this year because of the pandemic. The Jazz Festival, the world's biggest, counts more than two million visits annually.

Montreal Jazz Festival mascot at Place des Arts; Quebec and Montreal flags (photos by author)

Heritage events

Canada Day parade, Bury, Que. (photo by author)

Canada's rich multicultural heritage is celebrated by various annual heritage events across the country that have been affected this year by COVID-19. Some examples:

- Canada Day celebrations: Many July 1st celebrations across the country have been cancelled.

- Québec's Fête nationale: June 24th celebrations across the province have been cancelled.
- St. Patrick's Day Parade, Montreal: On March 13, the United Irish Societies announced the postponement of the St. Patrick's parade in Montreal, an event that has never been cancelled in its 196-year history.

Massed Bands, Glengarry Highland Games, Maxville, Ont. (photo by author)

Fireworks at Royal Military Tattoo, Edinburgh, Scotland (photo by author)

- Glengarry Highland Games, Maxville, Ontario: On April 22, the organizers announced that the 73rd edition of the Glengarry Highland Games, North America's biggest, has been cancelled and will instead be presented in the summer of 2021.
- Caribbean Carnival, Toronto: It was announced on April 9 that the Toronto Caribbean Carnival (formerly Caribana) which, for the past 52 years, has delivered an exciting summer festival featuring elaborate costumes, Caribbean music and food, will be cancelled for this year.
- Royal Edinburgh Military Tattoo, Edinburgh, Scotland: On April 1, it was announced that the 70th anniversary edition of this world-famous event was cancelled.

Miscellaneous events

Various other events, both in Canada and overseas, were also victims of the COVID-19 pandemic. Below are two examples:

- Pride Parade, Toronto: Mayor John Tory announced on March 31 that this year's parade is being cancelled. Pride Toronto is an annual event held to celebrate the diversity of the LGBT community in the Greater Toronto Area.
- Oberammergau Passion Play, Germany: It was announced on March 24 that this once-a-decade event would be postponed to 2022 (yes, two full years from now). This popular event, which my wife and I had the privilege of attending in 2000, has a most fascinating and timely history:

Having already lost 80 of their own to the plague, the villagers of

Passion Play theatre, Oberammergau, Germany (photo by author)

Oberammergau pledged to perform the Passion of Jesus Christ – his suffering, death, and resurrection – every tenth year, in order that no one else might die. So goes the historical legend of the origins of the Oberammergau Passion Play, an almost four-century-old tradition that takes place once every 10 years. The year of the pledge was 1633, not 2020. The Pest – German for plague – was the so-called "Black Death," not the COVID-19 pandemic. But, in an ironic twist, the 42nd Oberammergau season – set to run May 16 to October 4, 2020 – was postponed last week due to measures taken by local government authorities in response to the new coronavirus outbreak. (source: https://www.christianitytoday.com/news/2020/march/oberammergau-passion-play-cancel-COVID-19-coronavirus-germa.html)

Agricultural fairs

Brome Fair Ferris wheel and cattle parade (superimposed photos by author)

All agricultural fairs in Quebec are cancelled for this summer. This includes the very popular Eastern Townships fairs such as the Brome Fair, Ayer's Cliff Fair, Richmond Fair and my hometown's Expo Cookshire Fair, all of which have been annual fixtures, some for more than 150 years. These events, being highlights of the E.T. summer agri-social calendar, will be greatly missed.

Just as we were going to press, it was announced that Toronto's Canadian National Exhibition (CNE) – the mother of all Canadian fairs and exhibitions – would be cancelled this year. This popular annual event, that began in 1879 and

Canadian National Exhibition (photo by Bill Ivy)

Cookshire Fair (photo by author)

now draws more than a million visitors each summer, has been cancelled only once before in its long history: during the Second World War.

The 2020 Calgary Stampede has been cancelled for the first time since it became an annual event in 1923. The event avoided cancellation during the Great Depression, the Second World War and the flooding of the Bow and Elbow Rivers in 2013, but the COVID-19 pandemic has been judged too risky for an event that brings together hundreds of thousands of spectators.

Bronco riding, Calgary Stampede, Calgary, Alberta (photo by author)

Cabane à sucre: rite of spring

One of the spring events that I miss most is going to a sugar shack (or cabane-à-sucre as we call it here in Quebec). Historically, these gatherings were mostly limited to family and friends. But over the years, they have become public events and the menu has expanded to include some or all of the following: pea soup,

Maple sugar camp, Cookshire, Que. (photo by author)

pancakes, baked beans, sausages, bacon, ham, homemade pickles, scrambled eggs, "pigs' ears," sugar pie and ice cream – with many of the dishes smothered with fresh maple syrup.

The meal is served communal style in a large reception hall at rows of long tables. For most Quebecers, spring is not spring if you don't make at least one visit to a maple sugar bush. People are attracted by those special sights, sounds and smells – the sight of billowing white clouds of steam escaping through the cupola of the picturesque sugar shack, the drip...drip...drip sound of sap running into a galvanized bucket and the heavenly smell of freshly made maple syrup. And who can forget the taste of "sugar-on-snow" (some call it "taffy") – that delicious result of pouring hot syrup onto a trough of ice-cold snow? Unfortunately, all of these treats will have to wait until next year.

Filling the void

Leading musical artists from around the world have joined forces to offer their talents through virtual concerts.

On April 18, the World Health Organization and Global Citizen co-hosted a global on-air special to celebrate and support frontline healthcare workers. The program "One World: Together at Home" raised nearly $128 million in response to the COVID-19 crisis. The WHO website describes the event:

> Curated in collaboration with Lady Gaga, the broadcast included appearances by Andrea Bocelli, Céline Dion, Chris Martin, Eddie Vedder, Elton John, FINNEAS, Idris and Sabrina Elba, John Legend, Lang Lang, Lizzo, Maluma, Paul McCartney, Priyanka Chopra Jonas, Shah Rukh Khan and Stevie Wonder. This historic global event was hosted by TV show hosts Jimmy Fallon, Jimmy Kimmel and Stephen Colbert. It also featured real experiences from doctors, nurses and families around the world. Benefits from the concert will go to the COVID-19 Solidarity Response Fund, in addition to local and regional charities that provide food, shelter and healthcare to those that need help most.

A similar televised Canadian event was held a week later, on April 26, and featured Canadian artists from across the country. "Stronger Together, Tous Ensemble" showcased an impressive cast of celebrities and music artists, including Céline Dion (who also appeared on One World), Shania Twain, Bryan Adams, Michael Bublé, Sarah McLachlan, Howie Mandel, Will Arnett, Jason Priestley, Margaret Atwood, Russell Peters, and Alessia Cara. More than $6 million was raised for Food Banks Canada.

Coping with the closures and cancellations

People mourn the absence (through cancellation, postponement or temporary closure) of their favourite cultural/entertainment events and facilities. Below some of them share their comments:

My Stratford theatre tickets for the spring (and probably summer too), and my Kitchener-Waterloo Symphony ticket this month are cancelled. I shudder to think of the implications this has on performers' incomes and cultural organizations in general. Will they survive this interruption in their industry? (Carol Alguire)

Due to the pandemic, some entertainers have been holding mini-concerts in their homes and we get to see them on television or Facebook. Two such artists are Garth Brooks and Keith Urban. This is extremely uplifting to me in this time of uncertainty. (Karen Jackson)

Bell, our Internet provider, dropped the charge for watching movies so we immediately recorded a number of them that were available. Everything from "To Kill a Mockingbird" to "Edna's Bloodline." We have enough to allow us to watch movies well into May. So now we watch movies three times a week with popcorn, something we really didn't do before. (David and Margaret Gussow)

On April 4 a bull auction in Saskatoon was conducted almost entirely through online bidding due to the pandemic. Videos had been taken of the bulls walking around in their winter yard here, so bidders could see them as if they were there at the auction site. Richard watched the whole thing unfold on the computer, and could follow the bidding in real time. Seventy-four bulls were sold, including 10 from our farm. Could this be the way things will be done in the future? (Diane Keet)

Chapter 10
Financial frenzy

Piggybank (istockphoto.com – credit malerapaso)

Although COVID-19 is first and foremost a health crisis, it also has far-reaching financial implications. No component of the Canadian economy escaped unscathed. Personal piggybanks were quickly emptied. Businesses' balance sheets turned from black to red. Stock markets spiralled out of control. Seniors watched helplessly as their retirement nest eggs shrank before their cataract-coated eyes. And Canada saw its gross domestic product projections plummet.

The concurrence of so many negative circumstances was unprecedented. So was the government's response. Assuring Canadians that it would do "whatever it takes," it announced – on an almost daily basis – an ever-expanding series of relief measures.

This chapter briefly outlines the above-mentioned financial challenges and some of the remedies that were implemented.

Piggybank plunder

The sudden loss of employment by millions of Canadians is having immediate and important effects on their already precarious personal financial situations. Even before the crisis hit, many families and individuals were living paycheque to paycheque. As well, they were saddled with high levels of debt due to the prevailing low interest rates. Despite financial planners' and experts' recommendation that consumers keep enough cash on hand to pay for at least three months of groceries, utilities and mortgage payments, this is only a pipe dream for many. And so the poor piggybank has been quickly drained of its loonies and toonies.

Business belly blows

The COVID-19 pandemic has had an enormous impact on Canadian businesses of all sizes but most especially small independent businesses. From an April 23 survey, the 110,000-member Canadian Federation of Independent Business discovered that:

- On the Canada Emergency Wage Subsidy: 29% [of respondents] are saying that it will help them avoid further layoffs or recall staff, 37% are saying it will not help them, while 21% are unsure.
- On the Canada Emergency Business Account: 1 in 5 businesses don't think they will qualify for a CEBA loan.
- Only 20% [of businesses] are fully open, 30% do not have cash flow to pay April bills and 39% are worried about permanent closure.
- 32% of those who have had to close are unsure if they will be able to reopen.
- 25% say they can survive less than a month under current conditions.
- 86% believe the government should make emergency money available to businesses that have been hard hit by COVID-19 to cover their fixed costs.
- 56% said they have no more capacity to take on debt during this emergency.
- The average cost of COVID-19 on small business so far is $214,915. (source: https://www.cfib-fcei.ca/en/research/survey-results/investigating-the-impact-of-COVID-19-on-independent-business)

The bear awakes

After more than ten years of burgeoning bull markets, the bear emerged early from winter hibernation to suddenly wrest control of stock fortunes. As illustrated in the table and charts following, both the New York Stock Exchange and the Toronto Stock Exchange benchmark indices lost more than a third of their value (as compared to their record highs recorded in February) when they hit historic lows on March 23. The main cause of the stock market crash was, of course, the COVID-19 crisis, but an oil price war between Saudi Arabia and Russia didn't help.

Bear market warning sign (istockphoto.com – credit mphillips007)

The stock market crash

Stock index	Record high	Record low	% drop
NYSE Dow Jones	29,551 (Feb. 12, 2020)	18,543 (Mar. 23, 2020)	37%
Toronto TSX	17,994 (Feb. 20, 2020)	11, 228 (Mar. 23, 2020)	37%

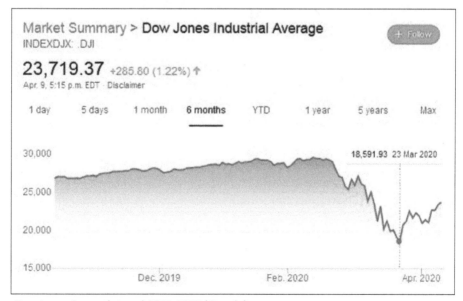

Dow Jones 6-month trend 2019-2020 (Google)

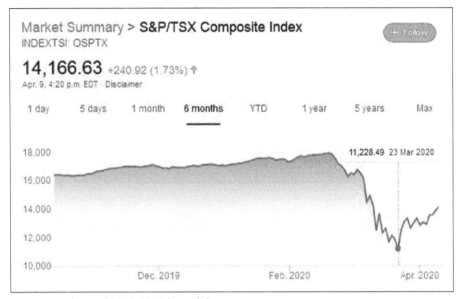

TSX 6-month trend 2019-2020 (Google)

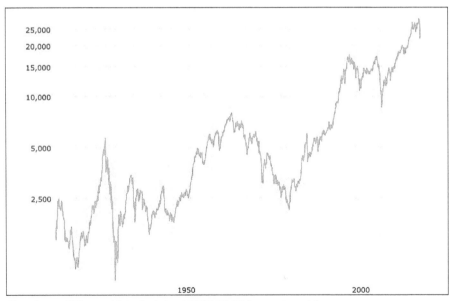

Dow Jones 100-year historical chart 2020 04 22 (macrotrends)

Sinking funds

For seniors, the COVID-19 crisis gives new meaning to the financial term "sinking funds" as they watched the value of their mutual funds plummet faster than a Usain thunderBolt. But, as my financial advisor always says, "Don't worry . . . they'll come back up . . . Remember, you're in it for the long term." That may be well and good, but will we all still be around for the long term? Nevertheless, he is right – historically, the markets have always bounced back, as indicated in the 100-year chart opposite.

Pessimistic projections

An April 15 announcement by the Bank of Canada painted a less-than-pretty picture of Canada's economic situation:

> The Canadian economy was in a solid position ahead of the COVID-19 outbreak, but has since been hit by widespread shutdowns and lower oil prices. One early measure of the extent of the damage was an unprecedented drop in employment in March, with more than one million jobs lost across Canada. Many more workers reported shorter hours, and by early April, some six million Canadians had applied for the Canada Emergency Response Benefit . . . The outlook is too uncertain at this point to provide a complete forecast. However, Bank analysis of alternative scenarios suggests the level of real activity was down 1-3% in the first quarter of 2020, and will be 15-30% lower in the second quarter than in fourth-quarter 2019. CPI inflation is expected to be close to 0% in the second quarter of 2020 . . . Canada's GDP shrank by 9% in March and 2.6% during the first quarter of 2020. (Bank of Canada)

Worker relief

An ever-expanding series of programs and measures were announced by the federal government, beginning with the Canada Emergency Response Benefit. Its goal is to assist those who have stopped working because of COVID-19 by providing temporary income support of $500 a week for up to 16 weeks. It is available to Canadian residents who are at least 15 years old; are not eligible for employment insurance (EI) regular or sickness benefits; had income of at least $5,000 in 2019 or in the 12 months prior to the date of their application; and expect to be without employment or self-employment income for at least 14 consecutive days in the initial four-week period. For subsequent benefit periods, they expect to have no employment or self-employment income.

Business relief

Businesses also benefitted from the government's largesse. First among the many initiatives introduced was the Canada Emergency Wage Subsidy. Its purpose is to support employers that are hardest hit by the pandemic, and to protect the jobs that Canadians depend on. The subsidy covers 75% of an employee's wages – up to $847 per week – for employers of all sizes and across all sectors that have suffered a drop in gross revenues of at least 15% in March, and 30% in April and May. The program applies for a 12-week period, from March 15 to June 6, 2020. The goal of the program is to help businesses keep workers on the payroll and to rehire those who were already let go.

The fact that the relief programs would be in force for months reflected Prime Minister Trudeau's warning on April 8 that Canadians should expect to stay home with businesses closed for months, rather than weeks.

Economic relief

In addition to its direct support of workers and businesses, the government made significant moves to shore up the country's economy. Among them were the following actions:

- At a press conference on March 13, Finance Minister Bill Morneau, flanked by Stephen Poloz, governor of the Bank of Canada, and Jeremy Rudin, superintendent of financial institutions, declared "We're going to do whatever it takes to support and stabilize our economy." Poloz announced a surprise interest-rate cut, dropping the benchmark rate by a half-point for the second time in less than two weeks. For his part, Rudin lowered the amount of capital that the country's biggest banks must keep in reserve to reduce the risk of default. That will allow lenders such as the country's banks to put more money in play.

- On March 27, Morneau and Bank of Canada Governor Stephen Poloz held a news conference in Ottawa following the central bank's announcement that it is once again lowering its key interest rate, to 0.25%, in response to the economic impact of the ongoing COVID-19 crisis.

(Complete details of Canada's Economic Response Plan are available at https://www.canada.ca/en/department-finance/news/2020/03/canadas-COVID-19-economic-response-plan-support-for-canadians-and-businesses.html)

World economic actions

Other countries have also taken very strong economic action to counter the devastating negative effects of COVID-19. Following are three examples:

- Lawmakers in the U.S. agreed on a stimulus package worth $2 trillion in an attempt to keep the teetering U.S. economy from falling into a recession. Among its provisions was a one-time payment to all Americans of $1,200 per person, or $3,000 for a family of four.

- Germany, the largest economy in the E.U., approved a coronavirus stimulus package worth over €750 billion ($814 billion), marking the first instance of the German government taking on new debt since 2013. The fund, which Chancellor Angela Merkel's cabinet agreed upon, includes €600 billion for business loans and to buy direct stakes in companies and €156 billion in debt to finance higher social spending. Finance Minister Olaf Scholz said the economy would need support even after the virus was contained.

- France's finance minister unveiled a €45 billion aid package for businesses and workers, adding that more economic support was still to come.

  (source: https://www.dw.com/en/coronavirus-what-aid-packages-have-governments-agreed/a-52908669 March 25)

Financial comments

People share their comments, opinions and observations on the financial situation:

Our economy is going to suffer tremendously and will take years to recover. This truth causes anxiety among young adults, as they struggle with jobs, relationships, wedding plans and new babies. (Carol Alguire)

At this critical time in the health and employment crisis, I find it extraordinary that Bell has taken the opportunity to increase my Internet fee by $6.00 a month. We've all been told by governments, during this COVID-19 emergency, to turn to the Internet for information, continuing education and communication with our families. Considering the magnitude of unemployment, is this the right time for our communications giant to put profit before public service? (George Dunbar, letter to the Editor of the Toronto Star, March 23)

Personal finances and the economy are frightening. But our financial advisor says "not to worry." We rely on his knowledge and experience. (Elaine Fraser)

Nothing much has changed except that we have fewer expenses – less gas for the car, no more eating at restaurants and no more visits to family and friends. It's harder to find cash because the nearest financial institution is some 15 km away. However, it's not too much of a problem since most merchants prefer card payment – in fact some don't even accept cash. (Jacques Crépeau and Ginette Arcand)

In life-and-death matters such as the COVID-19 pandemic, a focus on financial matters can seem misplaced. But for the world's poor, the financial impacts of COVID-19 can be devastating and far more immediate (Michael Tarazi, Consultative Group to Assist the Poor, www.cgap.org)

Chapter 11
Necessity is the mother of innovation

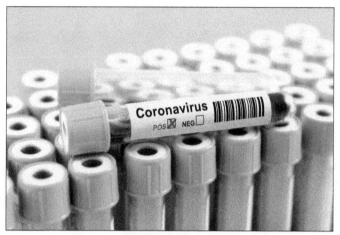

Coronavirus test vials (istockphoto.com – credit anilakkus)

Researchers are among the hidden heroes of our society. In the scientific laboratories of academia, government and industry, they quietly search for solutions, often spending years to perfect a product or process. That is the timeline in normal times. But in COVID-19 times like this, lead times are measured in weeks, not years. As the coronavirus accelerated its advance across the globe, researchers, manufacturers and distributors sped up their efforts to counter it. They realize that the seriousness of the situation means that there is no time to lose.

It is important to recognize that not all research takes place in well-funded facilities and not all researchers are scientists or professors. As illustrated below, some breakthrough discoveries are being made by ordinary individuals and are being conceived in basements, kitchens and garages.

The reader is cautioned that the inclusion of information concerning the devices and processes described below is in no way meant to imply endorsement but rather to serve as examples of possible solutions, subject to the necessary testing and required approvals.

Testing . . . testing . . . testing

One of the earliest challenges related to COVID-19 was the availability of efficient test kits. Many of those initially available were not readily portable and were complicated to use. Because of the rapidly increasing demand for testing, the process needed to be simpler and quicker. Enter Spartan Bioscience. Their portable test kit is described as follows in an April 13 report:

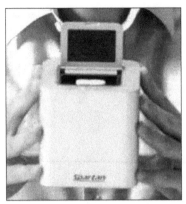 

Spartan Bioscience COVID-19 test kit (Spartan)

Ottawa-based Spartan Bioscience has developed a coffee cup-sized rapid -testing device for COVID-19. Health Canada has approved the Ottawa company's new technology that is aimed at expanding the country's COVID-19 test capacity. Spartan Bioscience was one of the companies to receive federal funds announced in mid-March to help in the fight against the coronavirus pandemic. It adapted its portable DNA test kits to a similar hand-held, cube-shaped device that could do quick tests (30 minutes or less) for the novel coronavirus outside of laboratories in settings such as airports, border crossings and remote communities. (source: cbc.ca)

In the United Kingdom, at Cranfield University, a very different kind of coronavirus detection process is being researched.

Researchers are working on a new test to detect SARS-CoV-2 in the wastewater of communities infected with the virus. The wastewater-based epidemiology (WBE) approach could provide an effective and rapid way to predict the potential spread of novel coronavirus pneumonia (COVID-19) by picking up on biomarkers in feces and urine from disease carriers that enter the sewer system. (source: Cranfield University. "Wastewater test could provide early warning of COVID-19." ScienceDaily, 31 March 2020. www.sciencedaily.com/ releases/2020/03/200331092713.htm.)

Personal protective equipment (PPE)

Personal protective equipment consists of gowns, gloves, masks and facial protection. As the pandemic progressed, there was much concern about the availability and quality of various types of PPE. Among the most critical were those required for the face protection of health care workers. A Montreal team came up with a very creative solution that is described in this report:

A Montreal surgeon has teamed up with a hockey equipment manufacturer and a company that specializes in air quality to produce protective hoods for Quebec healthcare workers tackling the COVID-19 pandemic. Dr. René Caissie, of Montreal's Sacré-Coeur Hospital, CCM Hockey and Industrie Orkan, based in Saint-Hubert, Que., said their collaboration designed and produced the full-head protective hood in record time.

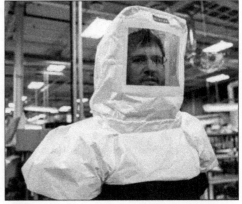

The hood completely covers a health-care worker's head and is powered by an air-purifying respirator, the collaborators said in a statement, and can be worn for several hours, reducing the number of times workers need to change their face protection. It was successfully tested at the Institut de Recherche en

A full-head protective hood (CNW Group/ CCM Hockey)

Santé et Securité du Travail (IRSST), a Quebec workplace safety research organization, and meets an even higher purity standard than that required for certification of N95 masks, the joint task force behind the new hood said.

Dr. Caissie, who along with being an oral and maxillofacial surgeon is a medical inventor, said he has witnessed first-hand the urgent need for medical professionals to be protected during their work fighting COVID-19. "With the rapidly declining quantity of personal protective equipment available in my work environment . . . I began to look for solutions," Dr. Caissie said. "I decided to participate in an effort to build our own equipment using materials that are readily available here in Montreal, so that this could move quickly and without having to depend on external factors more than absolutely necessary."

Dr. Caissie said he designed the prototype in his garage and then contacted CCM, the hockey equipment manufacturer, which had been looking for ways to use its expertise to help in the fight against COVID-19. With CCM on board, Dr. Caissie then contacted Industrie Orkan to help with the air-purifying respirator, a key component of the hood, which the company said it developed within 48 hours . . . The protective hood must first be approved for use by Quebec health authorities. Once that happens, CCM said it will produce as many as 150 of the hoods a day for as long there is demand. (source: https://montreal.ctvnews.ca/montreal-surgeon-teams-with-hockey-air-quality-companies-to-produce-protective-hoods-for-quebec-healthcare-workers-1.4893475?cache=ngyhfzxv%3FautoPlay%3Dtrue%3FautoPlay%3Dtrue%3FcontactForm%3Dtrue%3FclipId%3D68596)

A small-town entrepreneur from Manitoulin Island, Ont. wanted to make a difference and he certainly did. His invention is described below:

> Retired paramedic Bill Cranston of Mindemoya has created a novel method of delivering oxygen to COVID-19 patients while also potentially reducing the exhalation of viral droplets and airborne particles using an ordinary object with a series of one-way seals – a full-face snorkel mask. Mr. Cranston is a member of both the emergency committee and the patient advisory committee at Manitoulin Health Centre (MHC). He has been spending considerable time in his modest home workshop in recent months to help find solutions to make Manitoulin Island better prepared to fight the coronavirus. (source: https://www.manitoulin.ca/island-paramedic-re-engineers-snorkel-masks-to-deliver-oxygen-protect-front-line-medical-staff/, Apr. 8)

A Sherbrooke (Quebec) based multi-disciplinary team that included a professor from my alma mater, Bishop's University, has developed a revolutionary type of ventilator. The university describes the project in a newsletter to alumni:

> Bishop's University's Bruno Courtemanche, Coordinator of the Undergraduate Bishop's Earth Research Group (UBERG), was part of a Sherbrooke-based team of engineers, medical professionals, professors and graduate and undergraduate students that designed, built and tested a prototype medical ventilator in response to the COVID-19 crisis. The task was part of a challenge issued by the Montreal General Hospital Foundation and the McGill University

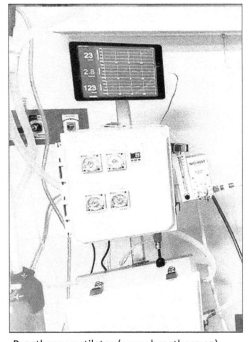

Breathere ventilator (www.breathere.ca)

114

Health Centre Research Institute that called on research teams to design simple, low-cost, easy-to-use ventilators that could be assembled quickly and easily if hospitals become overwhelmed and medical equipment becomes scarce. The "BreatHere" ventilator, as it's been named, is now awaiting approval from the government to move ahead with production. The team expects they can produce 1,000 machines in a week. (Bishop's University Alumni email)

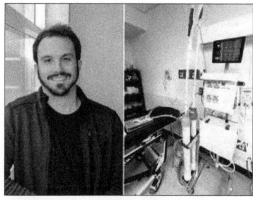

Bruno Courtemanche and Breathere ventilator (courtesy Bishop's University)

The mask question

In the midst of the pandemic, the mask debate rages on. "To wear or not to wear" – that was the Shakespearean question. In fact, that was but one of several questions. Should the mask, because of its low supply, be limited to health care workers only? Or should it be available to anyone who wants to wear one for their own protection? Furthermore, exactly who does the mask protect: the wearer or the persons with whom the wearer comes into contact? And, finally, what type/brand of mask provides the best protection?

N95 mask (istockphoto.com – credit Joe Cicak)

An Israeli company has developed a high-tech face mask that claims to actually **kill** viruses. New York-born Jeff Gabbay, a textile engineer and president of Argaman Technologies, provides details in the following report:

Thicker than a standard face mask, and with two ear loops, the Argaman mask has been accepted by the Hong Kong authorities as far more effective than the N95 respirator mask. Gabbay explains the difference:

"This mask doesn't filter; it's a deactivation device that actually kills bacteria and viruses." The green medical scrubs that the company produces could be found on any hospital ward – but with their nano-engineering, he says, they're far more than typical scrubs; they actually kill bacteria. Their advanced fibers make them odor-free – as attested by Jeff himself, a man who only needs to change his socks once a month! This technology has already helped miners survive weeks trapped underground in a Peruvian mine disaster with minimal infection . . . It all sounds like science fiction – can it really be true? Large-scale studies have yet to confirm his products' efficacy (and, according to standard medical protocol, thorough hygiene is still considered the primary means of infection control), but governments around the world seem to trust the existing data that Jeff's specially treated textiles can offer protection from coronavirus. With three million face masks being rushed from his production headquarters to Hong Kong, Argaman is scrambling to ramp up production as orders pour in. (source: https://mishpacha.com/the-man-behind-the-masks/)

A McGill University team is studying how to apply AI (artificial intelligence) to COVID-19 challenges. The lead professor explains:

Artificial intelligence and technologies could provide us substantial assistance in prevention, early detection, and management of COVID-19. This is the time we need to be more innovative than we have ever been, and make the best use of AI and the available technology to improve the situation and add value. In my team, we are working with international collaborators to use the power of AI and technology for prevention and management of COVID-19. (Samira Abbasgholizadeh-Rahimi, Assistant Professor, Department of Family Medicine, McGill University)

COVID-19 treatment

A team composed of researchers from more than 40 Canadian hospitals is looking at how a more-than-100-year-old therapy can be applied to the treatment of COVID-19. Their fast-tracked research is briefly summarized below:

In the global race to find a life-saving treatment for COVID-19, researchers are looking at whether the answer could be found in the blood plasma of recovered patients. When a person is infected with a virus, their immune system produces antibodies to help fight it off. Once the patient recovers, doctors can collect these helpful immune cells from the patient's blood plasma and inject them into sick patients to help them get better.

The approach is hardly new. Convalescent plasma therapy has been used to treat patients with SARS, Ebola, H1N1 as well as the Spanish flu epidemic of 1918. Now, a Canadian team is testing what happens when critically ill patients receive a recovered patient's immune cells. Similar testing is already underway in Asia and the United States, where a few very small studies have shown that patients who received doses of antibodies recovered enough to stop relying on ventilators. However, those studies are far from conclusive.

The new Canadian research could play a major role in establishing just how well the blood-based treatment works. Dr. Donald Arnold, an associate professor at McMaster University's department of medicine, said the study was assembled extremely quickly. "Now this would be a process that would normally take, you know, six to 12 months without exaggeration. We banded together and somehow managed to do it in the span of about seven days." (source: https://www.ctvnews.ca/health/coronavirus/can-antibodies-from-recovered-patients-help-people-with-COVID-19-1.4887510)

Real-time retooling

As was the case in World War II, Canadian factories were asked to retool and shift their production to critical medical equipment needed to fight the enemy. But unlike the war-time retooling, which was shrouded in secrecy, the COVID-19 conversions were proudly announced by the companies involved.

Stanfield's of Truro, Nova Scotia, famous for making underwear (including my boyhood combination underwear with the handy back door opening) has rehired laid-off workers to manufacture medical gowns. KDC/ONE of Knowlton in Quebec's Eastern Townships (where my nieces Lorelei, Jan and Alison work) quickly transformed their operations to produce hand sanitizer. Several new employees were hired to meet this new demand. Some other retooling examples are summarized below:

- Nearly 5,000 small Canadian businesses have offered to retool their factory floors to provide critical personal protective equipment for medical workers amid looming supply shortages.

- Brian's Custom Sports near Leamington, Ont., normally makes hockey goalie pads. Some of their clients have included NHL stars Felix Potvin and Patrick Roy. Now its employees are sewing stretcher sheets into disposable gowns for health-care workers.

- Dynamic Air Shelters has been manufacturing in Grand Bank, Newfoundland for nearly two decades. The company builds industrial shelters for the oil and gas industry, but has reverted to building emergency hospital and quarantine shelters.

- Lind Equipment, which produces lighting products for the military and mining operations, is now working to use their UV light systems to sterilize PPE in hospitals.

(source:https://www.ctvnews.ca/health/coronavirus/canadian-companies-retool-to-make-supplies-for-frontline-workers-1.4902712 – April 19)

Not all cases of retooling involve manufacturing plants. One example involves a member of my former parish church who responded to a late-March appeal for food assistance from Resilience Montréal, a day shelter located in Westmount, catering to the needs of Montreal's homeless population. With the COVID-19 situation, their centre had been forced to close its doors due to the small size of its premises. Tents and sanitary facilities were set up in a nearby square to help house the homeless people in the fight to keep the virus from spreading among that vulnerable part of the population.

Ann Gillard, a professional caterer, heard the appeal and, with the help of friends, sprang into action. Every week since, they prepare hundreds of sandwiches, gallons of cooked dishes (e.g., pasta and meat sauce, beef stew, meatballs in tomato sauce, beans and wieners) and loads of desserts, as well as various miscellaneous provisions, which she delivers to Resilience's temporary shelter on Cabot Square in Montreal. This significant volunteer effort does not go unappreciated, as witnessed by a handwritten sign posted by some of the beneficiaries.

Resilience Montréal – homeless appreciation sign (photo by Ann Gillard)

Physical distancing

One of the key measures to control the spread of COVID-19 is physical distancing, but one of the challenges is how to ensure that the 2-metre separation rule is followed. Two Montreal entrepreneurs have invented a device that would do just that in certain work environments:

> . . . working environments can make pose difficulties for compliance with physical distancing guidelines. After watching their employees navigate these issues, manufacturing veterans Jarred Knecht, John Soares and Steve Zimmermann joined forces and co-founded Social Distancer Technologies to create, with support from the National Research Council of Canada's Industrial Research Assistance Program (NRC IRAP), the Social Distancer, a wearable product designed to provide workers with a

Resilience Montreal volunteers and Ann Gillard (right) (photo courtesy Ann Gillard)

means to easily maintain a two-metre distance. . . The Social Distancer is a credit-card size, one-inch thick, patent-pending device that instantly calculates the distance between employees. It has three methods of alert

– visual, vibration and tone – to instantly notify employees. If employees are within 2.5 meters of one another, the device will flash red, vibrate and audibly alert the employees to move farther away. http://www.canadianminingjournal.com/news/covid-19-new-technology-for-physical-distancing-from-social-distancer/ April 23)

Social distancer unit (Social Distancer Technologies)

Early in the COVID-19 crisis, two former IBM colleagues and I discussed a more global solution to the problem through a combination of existing technologies. Following are excerpts of a proposal that we submitted to the government's Cabinet Committee on COVID-19.

We recommend that the Government of Canada immediately mandate a working group made up of representatives from smartphone manufacturers, cell phone service providers and independent software development companies to devise, develop and implement a "Physical Distancing Optimization and Monitoring (PDOM)" solution, whose characteristics could include, among others, the following:

- The real-time capability to automatically identify individuals not properly respecting the rules of physical distancing and to alert those individuals of their non-adherence

- The continuous collection of statistics that would allow the government and regional authorities to accurately measure the adherence level and to pin-point those geographic areas requiring remedial attention

- The short term objective would be to develop an MVP (Minimum Viable Product) solution, whatever form it may take (e.g. an "app", a device, or other). Of course, any solution must balance the urgent needs of the present pandemic with the protection of personal privacy.

Vaccine

Although research is being conducted on many different COVID-19 fronts simultaneously, the development of a vaccine for the virus represents the Holy Grail. A few of the more advanced projects of the hundreds underway worldwide are briefly described below:

- A University of Oxford coronavirus vaccine trial aims to have 500 people in testing by mid-May. The vaccine may be ready as soon as September. Two groups in the United States and one in China have already commenced human trials. Over 60 potential vaccine candidates and treatments for coronavirus are being developed in labs around the world, most in pre-clinical stages. U.S. company Moderna began clinical trials last month. The Oxford trial is one of just a handful that have progressed to the human testing phase, but more are coming online all the time. Existing clinical human trials from Moderna and Inovio are underway in the U.S. (source: April 17 https://techcrunch.com/2020/04/17/university-of-oxford-coronavirus-vaccine-trial-aims-to-have-500-people-in-testing-by-mid-may/)

- At this time, there is no vaccine authorized to protect against COVID-19. Nevertheless, clinical trials for COVID-19 vaccines are ongoing around the world, and Health Canada is working with vaccine developers and manufacturers to help expedite the development and availability of vaccines to prevent COVID-19. Health Canada is working to fast-track clinical trials for COVID-19 treatments. (source: https://www.canada.ca/en/health-canada/services/drugs-health-products/COVID19-clinical-trials.html)

- Drug companies join forces to develop vaccine. Competitors GlaxoSmithKline and Sanofi say they're working together on a vaccine to prevent COVID-19, hoping to leverage their combined manufacturing capacity. The companies say they hope their vaccine will be ready for human trials within months. (source: April 14 https://cmajnews.com/2020/04/09/coronavirus-1095847/)

- The Manitoba government announced on April 8 that it is spending $5 million on research into the novel coronavirus, including studies looking at whether or not the drug hydroxychloroquine can prevent – and possibly treat – COVID-19. (source: April 8 https://news.gov.mb.ca/news/index.html?item=47460&posted=2020-04-08)

- Prime Minister Trudeau announced on May 16 that the first Canadian clinical trials for a possible COVID-19 vaccine have been approved by Health Canada. The tests will take place at the Canadian Centre for Vaccinology (CCfV) at Dalhousie University in Halifax, N.S. (source: cbcnews.ca)

In conclusion, a wise word about vaccines from an expert:

The current COVID-19 pandemic underlines the importance of understanding the functioning of our bodies' immune system. Critics of vaccines can now see how lethal a world without a vaccine can be. It also highlights the fact that in a globalized society the development and distribution of vaccines for all infectious diseases is an essential cornerstone of a stable society. (Jörg Fritz, Associate Professor, Department of Microbiology and Immunology, McGill University)

Chapter 12
Our Mother's Voice

Antique Berliner gramophone, ca. 1919 (photo by author)

My mother was a loving, kind, caring person who had two distinctly different voices. Family outsiders knew her sweet, happy, smiling voice. But we kids, on the not-so-rare occasions when we misbehaved, came to know her other voice. Without warning, we would be subjected to a terrifying tongue-lashing tirade like no other – when the volume of her voice would go completely off the decibel scale!

Fast forward almost 100 years to today's COVID-19 crisis. Many contend that Mother (i.e. Mother Nature or Mother Earth) is speaking – even screaming – to us again through this pandemic. They echo the sentiment expressed some years ago by former Vice-President and climate crusader, Al Gore, who declared, in reference to the rising howls of extreme weather: "Can't you hear what Mother Nature is screaming at you?"

Are we listening?

Climate change activists like long-time Canadian environmentalist David Suzuki and Sweden's teenage climate conscience phenom, Greta Thunberg, don't believe that the world is listening as intently as it should. They remain skeptical that the issue will receive the attention that it needs.

In an April 17 Zoom call hosted by National Observer to discuss COVID-19 in the context of climate change, Suzuki offered the following observations:

> I have the sense that Mother Earth is saying, "Phew, thank God, these busy people are giving me a break," . . . The pause of human activity has allowed nature some rebound. . . it [the solution] doesn't mean trying to re-establish yesterday's economy, but redesigning it for the future, in a way that values the common fundamentals of life such as air, water and food. . . [There was] hopefulness about Trudeau's environmental commitment . . . But then he bought a pipeline . . . politics trumps the environment. . . [so] massive efforts on the part of the public are critical . . . [such as] the half-million demonstrators who accompanied Greta Thunberg in the global march for climate action this past September. . . the climate crisis is, in orders of magnitude, a greater threat [than COVID -19]. The COVID crisis is a crisis for human beings, but the climate crisis is a crisis for life on the planet. (Source: https://www.nationalobserver.com/2020/04/17/news/david-suzuki-applying-COVID-19s-lessons-climate-change)

For her part, Greta Thunberg, in a March 24 interview with Thomson Reuters Foundation, stated that the swift and far-ranging economic and social shifts being

Montreal Climate March, September 27, 2019 (photo by Kira-Marie Lazda)

brought in to stem the coronavirus pandemic showed that the rapid action needed to curb climate change was also possible.

Maybe the dolphins have not returned to the canals of Venice, but there is no doubt that the COVID-19 pandemic has already had some very significant positive effects on the environment. In Venice, the water in the canals is now clear (albeit because the bottom sediment is no longer being churned up by boat traffic). And in Wuhan, China, it is said that residents can hear birds singing again due to the reduction in traffic noise.

However, the big question is whether the benefits being experienced in the heat of this crisis will be sustained when the economy gets back on its feet and "normalcy" returns.

Emissions reductions

Satellite images from NASA and the European Space Agency have shown that the world's major industrial regions such as China, Europe and the United States have experienced dramatic reductions in pollution since the onset of the COVID-19 crisis. The following article and images provide details:

> The coronavirus outbreak has seen widespread changes in human behaviour, encouraging companies to alter everyday operations by suggesting employees work from home, which is reducing congestion and enhancing air quality. NASA's Earth Observatory recently released satellite images of China highlight the dramatic reduction in pollution, in particular in nitrogen dioxide (NO_2), that occurred this year. Nitrogen dioxide is emitted by motor vehicles, industrial facilities and power plants. This reduction was initially identified around Wuhan, but rapidly spread across China as millions of people have been quarantined and forced to make dramatic alterations to their everyday routines. (source: https://www.birmingham.ac.uk/research/perspective/COVID-19-climate-change.aspx)

A National Geographic article describes how the greatly reduced travel in the United States during the pandemic has resulted in a corresponding reduction of emissions:

> Transit-related emissions seem to be taking a nosedive in the U.S. too. According to Trevor Reed, an analyst at transportation research firm INRIX, U.S. passenger vehicle traffic was down by about 38% early last week. . . . So the COVID-19 outbreak and the resulting social isolation actually decreased total fossil fuel consumption caused by vehicular traffic in the U.S. (Source: Madelaine Stone, "Carbon Emissions Are Falling Sharply Due to Coronavirus. But Not for Long," National Geographic, April 3, 2020, www.nationalgeographic.com/.)

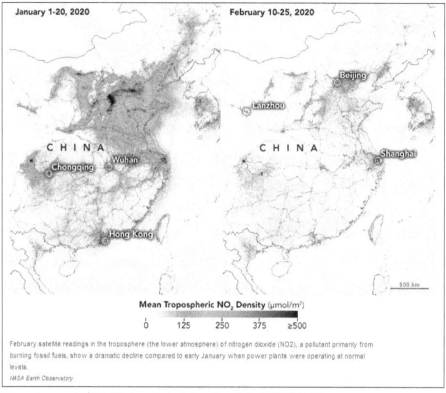

Mean tropospheric NO2 density in China, Jan.-Feb. 2020 (NASA)

Don't celebrate yet

However, as positive as these developments appear to be, it is not time to pop open the champagne in celebration. The following excerpts from a Voices of Youth blog entry give cause for concern:

> Photos of reduced smog in China, unpolluted canals in Italy, and wild animals roaming the streets in the United States have been shared all over Facebook, Instagram, and Twitter over the past few weeks, helping give hope to a demoralized global population . . . [but] the pandemic has led to the abandonment of many environmental sustainability programs – in the United States, smaller municipalities have halted recycling programs due to the risks associated with the spread of the virus. There has also been an increase in medical waste – much of the personal protective equipment that healthcare professionals are using can only be worn once before being disposed of . . . Furthermore, many have predicted that following mandatory lockdowns, countries will be focused on restarting their economies by funding industrial activities, while individuals will want to travel . . . These actions could reverse what beneficial environmental effects have arisen from the pandemic

response. (source: https://www.voicesofyouth.org/blog/unexpected-environmental-consequences-COVID-19)

An article on Earth Day's website expands on the implications of additional medical waste mentioned above:

> Given that surgical masks are supposed to be worn for no longer than one day, their disposal – along with that of empty hand sanitizer bottles and soiled tissue papers – is leading to a massive trail of clinical waste in the environment. The adverse effects of such clinical debris are far-reaching. Once these are left discarded in an animal's natural habitat – be it land or water – this may cause animals to mistake this trash for food, which could lead to entanglement, choking, ingestion and death. (source: https://earth.org/COVID-19-unmasking-the-environmental-impact/)

Red alert

One of the greatest challenges facing climate change scientists and activists is making the world (i.e., its governments and its people) realize that this is an emergency. One climate activist expresses it very succinctly:

> In the past, one of my biggest challenges working on climate change and climate change solution is trying to get people to understand that there's an emergency and there's something we need to do. Because people have been so comfortable in their daily lives, it's hard to see that there's an emergency . . . it's taken a pandemic for people to pay attention to the environment, because it's an "invisible" emergency that people can't necessarily see in the present . . . People need to listen to climate scientists the same way they are listening to those who are dealing with the pandemic . . . it's the jurisdictions that listened to scientists early that are handling the pandemic best. (Curtis Hull, P. Eng., Climate Change Connection)

Balancing act

Governments have long been hampered from taking definitive action on the environment for fear of upsetting the economic apple cart. In that context, Canada recently attempted to do something that potentially will help both. Walking a thin line between the need to assist Alberta's energy sector and the desire to protect the environment, Prime Minister Trudeau on April 17 announced support work in the oil and gas sector by spending $1.7 billion to help clean up "orphaned wells." He maintained that restoring abandoned oil and gas wells is "good for the environment, for landowners who have to contend with them, and for thousands of workers the effort will employ."

Balancing act (istockphoto.com – credit orla)

Save the planet. Save lives.

One less-discussed aspect related to climate change is the toll that air pollution takes in terms of human lives lost because of it. Logan Mitchell of the University of Utah department of atmospheric sciences explains:

> Ultimately, air quality improvements could save more lives than COVID-19 claims – if we continue with habits like teleworking and choose to invest in green technology as we rebuild the economy . . . According to estimates from the World Health Organization, exposure to outdoor air pollution causes 4.2 million premature deaths per year. Those deaths could outweigh mortality from COVID-19, depending on the disease's ultimate toll. (source: https://www.deseret.com/indepth/2020/3/30/21191391/COVID-19-coronavirus-utah-pollution-clean-air-pandemic-china-shut-down-working-from-home)

Comments from an expert

> For decades, we have tried – and failed – to act on climate change. It seemed as though real progress was impossible and that we were locked into a zombie walk into the future. Governments seemed to care about profits much more than people. However, the response to COVID-19 has turned that upside-down. It shows that most governments of the world are ready to put the welfare of people first. This is great news for our future, and that of our planet. We will need to push our governments to keep working for people, once we have made it through the COVID-19 pandemic. (Eric Galbraith, Full Professor, Department of Earth and Planetary Sciences, McGill University)

Comments from the public gallery

Less air pollution in the world is having a positive effect on the ozone layer. New wildlife sightings locally – a peregrine falcon spotted on our chimney top and a wild turkey seen on our street in Dorval! (Elaine Fraser)

Imagine what could be achieved if as much global effort were to be focused on addressing the global climate change crisis – an existential threat – as is being focused on fighting COVID-19. (Jim Fraser and Carol Alette)

We notice, looking out into our back yard, a greatly increased number of birds visiting. From blue jays, to juncos, to robins and cardinals. (David and Margaret Gussow)

Each morning we stand by the patio door and watch the birds and squirrels and numerous species we've rarely seen as the traffic stopped, the gyms closed and animals roam about asking themselves what happened! (Lorenzo Tartamella)

We birdwatch every day and record the species we see. Earlier in the season, we installed a dozen birdhouses for tree swallows and black-capped chickadees. Because we have more time to work on the grounds, we pruned the plum trees and have enlarged the garden space. (Jacques Crépeau and Ginette Arcand)

I feel that the isolation of people and shutdown of many businesses will give the environment a chance to recover somewhat. I personally plan to use the car less, buy more locally and to grow and make as much of my own food as possible. (Tracie Dougherty)

The environment around the world, especially in China and Italy, and even our own country of Canada, is showing a big improvement in the atmosphere, as the ozone layer is lifted. Will the lesser use of cars, trucks, planes and ships continue when the pandemic is over, so we can maintain a better climate for future generations? I hope that this may be a positive outcome from COVID 19. (Carol Alguire)

It appears that "Mother Nature" is much more dangerous to us than we are to ourselves. I wonder how many are claiming this to be an "Act of God?" Certainly, a calamity, in any case. Mother Nature has a way of reminding us that human life is wonderful, exciting, fearful, mystical, dangerous, regrettable, mysterious, woeful, joyful, rewarding, adventuresome and always final. (George Dunbar)

Happy 50th Earthday!

As I am putting the final touches on this chapter, I realize that today, April 22, 2020 is the 50th anniversary of the first Earth Day in 1970. A quick Google search revealed a most interesting and thought-provoking article in the Seattle Times, excerpts of which are reproduced below:

2020 Earth Day (istockphoto.com – credit onurdongel)

The Seattle Times headline on Seattle's first Earth Day, on April 22, 1970, was prescient. So much so, it could have been written on this year's 50th anniversary of Earth Day. "Pollution to Overheat Earth, Says Expert" was the headline stripped across the top of Page One. "The release of increasing quantities of carbon dioxide and thermal pollution into the atmosphere threatens to change global weather and melt the Antarctic ice cap, flooding wide areas," the story reported. Fifty years later, the pace toward warming predicted in the story . . . continues unchecked. . . Perhaps now some of the changes people have been forced to undertake because of the pandemic can take root even after the virus passes . . . from working at home more, to flying and driving less, to growing and cooking more food at home . . . Climate strategist Don Sampson sees a

Air pollution from smokestacks (istockphoto.com – credit Maxim Shmakov)

message in the coronavirus calamity coinciding with this half-century Earth Day anniversary. "This is definitely a shot across the bow from Mother Nature, telling us it is time to wake up, humans, this is just a precursor of what will happen," said Sampson, a traditional chief of the Walla Walla Tribe. . . "Mother Nature is talking to us. We better start listening to her." (source: https://www.seattletimes.com/seattle-news/environment/what-coronavirus-tells-us-about-climate-change-on-earth-days-50th-anniversary/)

Chapter 13
On the front line

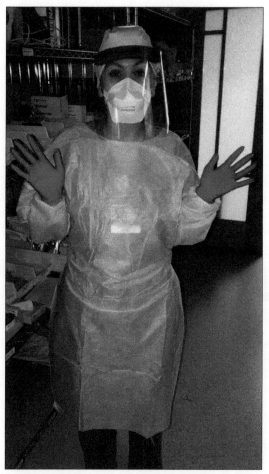

Nurse Delaney Callahan in full COVID-19
protective gear, April 2020 (courtesy Delaney
Callahan)

The fight against the COVID pandemic has often been likened to a war. As in any war, it is the front line that bears the biggest brunt of the battle. This chapter is a salute to the army of angels that are at the forefront of the fight.

The advance party

For weeks before the first patient is admitted for treatment of COVID-19, an advance party of government epidemiologists, health care professionals and hospital administrators are busy preparing for the expected onslaught. Among their tasks are the following:

- Free up hospital beds and operating rooms for eventual COVID-19 patients
- Arrange to cancel or postpone scheduled elective surgeries
- Set up testing clinics and testing protocols, both in hospitals and elsewhere
- Obtain sufficient supplies of PPE and testing equipment
- Hire or redeploy the necessary additional staff

The COVID-19 ward

Because my late wife was a nurse, I am quite familiar with the high level of dedication that nurses apply to their job and the honour that they bring to their profession. As a result, I have a huge respect for nurses and, by extension, for all those working in health care. Therefore I salute the courageous women and men working in hospitals, clinics and any other care facility, especially those on the hospital wards who are charged with the care of COVID-19 patients.

My grandniece Delaney is a COVID-19 nurse working on the front line. Her mother provides some background:

> Delaney is an RN at one of the large Boston hospitals. Until two weeks ago, she had been working on a gyn-oncology post-surgical floor. Last week, that floor transitioned to a COVID unit and she has started taking care of patients infected with the virus. The workload has been manageable until now, but she has been warned that the surge will come within the next two weeks. (Pat Tracy-Callahan)

Below is Delaney's first-hand account, a few weeks later, of her experience working on a COVID-19 ward:

> As a healthcare worker in a major city hospital, my co-workers and I long ago anticipated that we would see some changes in our day-to-day practices as COVID-19 began to spread. Much like the rest of the world, we never could have anticipated how drastically our work would be altered. Under normal circumstances, I am an RN on a GYN-ONC floor, occasionally floating to other areas of the hospital when they have staffing needs. Due to limited scheduled surgeries, our floor closed at the end of March and for the past month I have been working as a staff nurse on a COVID Special Pathogens Unit.

I have a difficult time describing a typical day on a COVID unit because nothing about this can ever seem routine. On most days, I have been a staff nurse with an assignment of one to three patients, depending on the unit's census and acuity that day. Most of our floor has been working overtime each week to meet the staffing needs. Each shift on our unit has the staff nurses, a charge nurse, a resource nurse who can help with medications or repositioning patients, as well as multiple observers, whose sole job is to help us properly put on and take off our PPE in the safest way possible. I hadn't realized – until I almost entered a room without a face shield last week – how incredibly crucial the observers are to our safety.

From the moment I get my patient assignment, I am planning out my care for the day in order to minimize the number of times I have to enter the room, in order to minimize our own exposure and use of PPE. We try to cluster our care as much as possible, grouping together medication administration, assessments and smaller tasks. Every time I enter a patient room, I put on a disposable gown, an N95 mask (we wear surgical masks the rest of the time as soon as we step foot into the hospital), a large plastic face shield and gloves. Because everything that goes into the room has to be properly sanitized before bringing it out, we try to have every room equipped with what we need for vital signs, assessments and tests. Gone are the days of using my high quality (and monogrammed!) stethoscope. We now use disposable ones that stay in a patient's room until they leave. Inevitably I have moments that I forget to take a medication or a cup of water into a room, so I rely on calling a resource nurse for help to pass them to me through the door. This all relates back to conserving PPE. How I remove my equipment can be just as important as how I put it on. I take the gown, gloves, mask and shield off in a specific way to limit my exposure to anything contaminated. The gown and gloves are disposed of every time, but the N95 mask is placed in a container to use for the whole shift. The shield also gets sanitized after each use and is reused until it becomes visibly soiled or broken.

Because we can't just pop into a room to check on a patient at least every hour like my nursing brain tells me to do, I frequently use the iPads to video chat with patients. These check-ins are crucial, not only for patient safety, but also for helping our patients not feel so alone in all this. Without visitors, walks in the hall or simply being able to see your care team without masks and shields on, the hospital is a lonely place.

When it comes to actual patient care, our assessments have never been more important. If someone's oxygen saturation starts to decrease and I have to increase their supplemental oxygen even the smallest amount, I notify the doctor and team of COVID nurses. Unfortunately, we're all learning that when a COVID patient begins to decompensate, the situation can become scary very quickly, so we need everyone to be prepared for the worst-case scenario.

I never anticipated that, within my first 18 months of nursing, I would be on the front lines during a pandemic. There is so much that is frightening and unknown right now, but I try to appreciate the beautiful moments whenever I can. I've witnessed how courageous and caring my co-workers are. I've cheered in crowded hallways as patients are discharged from our floor to see their families for the first time in weeks. I've received a donated meal almost every shift I've worked because generous people want to give us one less thing to worry about. My friends and family have sent words of encouragement almost every day and seem to know when I need it most. I don't know when my work life will return to normal or if "normal" will even exist anymore, but I feel fortunate to continue to go to work each day and take care of others as best I can. (Delaney Callahan)

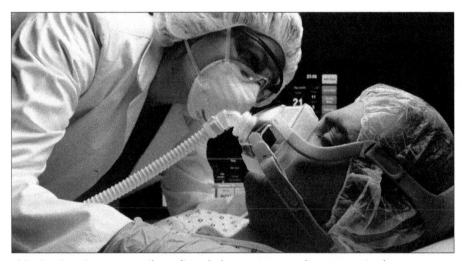

COVID-19 patient on ventilator (istockphoto.com – credit Juanmonino)

Intensive care

The term "intensive care" represents, at the same time, three different things – it is a place, it is people and it is a process. The place, of course, is the Intensive Care Unit (ICU) – that area of a hospital that is set aside to care for those who are the most seriously sick. The people are the medical personnel (doctors, nurses, technicians, etc.) who work in the ICU. And the process is the special care provided by those personnel.

In the COVID-19 context, Intensive Care, in all its aspects, plays a very critical role. This is where, by whom and how the most advanced cases of infection are treated. Although the majority of persons testing positive for the virus survive and recover – many of them not even requiring hospitalization – it is for the rest that the ICU is there. Sadly, there are those who do not survive in spite of the Herculean efforts of the ICU staff. Every premature death caused by COVID-19 is a tragedy for loved ones. One of my daughter's students recently shared with her that both his grandparents died of COVID-19 on the very same day. These situations also take an emotional toll on the health care workers who must nevertheless find the strength and courage to carry on the fight, day after day. It is little wonder that these angels of care have been recognized with parades and the banging of pots and pans.

Family physician perspective

Although they are not on the forward-most flank of the front-line, family physicians play an important and unique role in the COVID-19 war, as explained by my own family doctor:

> With the onset of the current COVID-19 crisis, there was an obligation of every general practitioner, be it in solo or group practice, to establish a protocol for the evaluation and recommendations for patients potentially at risk of having the virus. Interestingly, the priority was not to treat these patients, but to **prevent** them from coming to the office. Like most clinics, we have many vulnerable patients (elderly, chronic medical conditions, immunosuppression due to illnesses or treatment, etc.). If these patients were exposed to the virus, then the complications could potentially be harmful or deadly. Another risk would be for the medical/administration staff. If a staff member were to become positive, then the entire clinic would have to self-isolate for 14 days, forcing the clinic to close.
>
> Every potential patient would be screened for risk, initially based on travel (or exposure to someone who travelled) to endemic areas plus symptoms of fever, cough or shortness of breath. Any patient who satisfied the criteria was told to get tested (by phoning the appropriate number) or to go directly to the hospital if they were very symptomatic.
>
> For patient visits to our clinic, all non-urgent cases were postponed. To minimize exposure, the majority of visits were done over the phone or via telemedicine. If patients had to come in, then strict precautions were followed, protecting both the patient and the clinic staff. Understandably, this situation has caused stress for both the patients and for the medical staff. In addition, family members of the medical staff are constantly concerned regarding possible transmission at home. As medical director of a family medicine clinic, the approach is fairly straightforward. Despite being a dynamic, evolving situation, the best way to successfully overcome this is to develop and follow the appropriate protocols. These include a screening questionnaire for patients who call, following strict protection for patient visits, maintaining social distancing and washing hands within the clinic. In addition, being understanding and reassuring with patients and staff will facilitate the management of this crisis. (Dr. Paul Piechota, Clinique Access Med)

Medical specialist perspective

Naturally, in the midst of the pandemic the role of hospitals is especially focused on the treatment of COVID-19 patients. However, there many other patients requiring the care of medical specialists in a multiplicity of specialized hospital departments. My neurologist is one such specialist who shares how the pandemic has affected her practice:

> Most physicians, like myself, who follow patients with chronic illness have had to adapt our usual way of work to accommodate the era of COVID-19. We are now calling patients and managing appointments by phone or videoconference. For the most part, information can get translated but the whole other part of healing doesn't. It is hard to reassure patients by phone. We do our best but it isn't the same. Many patients are living alone and isolated for weeks – they may be anxious or depressed. Again, this is much harder to determine over the phone than in person. Of course, coronavirus is on everyone's mind and a source of anxiety in particular for the elderly. Patients are relieved that we call them. They are happy to have a connection with us, but look forward to a time when they can see us in person.
>
> Something else that has changed tremendously is our interaction with other health care workers. We no longer have meetings in person, but rather all by Zoom. At first it was almost fun to use the technology, but now we realize that conversations are often choppy because of poor internet connection and two persons may talk at once without realizing it. Also, I have found that attending meetings by Zoom or other such technologies is much more tiring than meeting face to face. The days are longer – more meetings, more planning, more changing our ways. We are adapting but certainly miss the simplicity of how things were. (Anne-Louise Lafontaine, Head of Neurology, McGill University Health Centre)

Often we tend to think of the "front line" as being limited to the doctors, nurses and other health care workers who directly care for those afflicted with the coronavirus. But, in reality, it includes many more. To name just a few: security officers and first responders, supply chain workers and other essential service workers. In the end, we are really **all** on the front line because it is our individual actions that are key to stopping the spread of the virus.

The supply chain

During this crisis, we hear a lot about the "supply chain" and the need to keep it operating in spite of all the difficulties and challenges. But what exactly does the term imply? A quick Internet search uncovered a very clear definition:

- A supply chain is a network between a company and its suppliers to produce and distribute a specific product or service.

- The entities in the supply chain include producers, vendors, warehouses, transportation companies, distribution centers, and retailers.
- The functions in a supply chain include product development, marketing, operations, distribution, finance, and customer service.
- Supply chain management results in lower costs and a faster production cycle. (source: https://www.investopedia.com/terms/s/supplychain.asp)

In understanding the above terms, it becomes clear why the supply chain constitutes such an essential service and why its workers represent a critical extension of the front line. Therefore, in the current COVID-19 war context, grocery store workers, warehouse workers, factory workers and truck drivers are all front-line soldiers.

View from a grocery store cashier

Working at a grocery store during this pandemic has been stressful, but I appreciate the fact that the owners, the Sharpes, have taken steps to make it a pretty safe place. We have a protective glass in front of us at the tills and a hand washing station for customers before they enter the store. We constantly wash our hands, the counters and the debit machines to prevent the spread. Customers line up outside, 6 ft. apart, before entering the store. For the most part, customers have been very understanding with the new rules and the quantity limitations on some products such as certain cleaning items. But there have been times where customers would yell and get upset because we didn't have enough toilet paper or Lysol wipes! I had an incident where a customer yelled at me insisting that there was no sign indicating a limit on hand sanitizer and tried to take five bottles. There actually was a sign but they chose to ignore it and disobey the rules. Because the environment has been very fast paced, it has taken time to adjust to it over these past few weeks. However, I appreciate having a job and getting more experience. Things have calmed down lately and I am looking forward to things getting back to normal soon. (Makeda Smith)

Grocery cashier Makeda Smith working behind Plexiglas separator (courtesy Carol Rand)

View from a trans-border trucker

Transportation plays a key role in the efficient operation of the supply chain. Truckers, then, are part of the army of essential workers, regardless of the type of goods they are hauling. My cousin Harry, an owner-operator long-distance trans-border trucker for more than 30 years, shares his experiences and observations:

Long haul trans-border trucking (photo by Harry Bellam)

My first trip in April was to St. Joseph, Missouri. The nice thing about that trip was no lineup at the USA border. That night we got to Perry, Michigan. When we arrived, the restaurant was closed and showers were also not available. The next morning, breakfast was a cold ham sandwich in the truck and a coffee from the store. After that, I managed to plan my trip better and would stop only

Mackay Bridge, Halifax, N.S. (istockphoto.com – credit shaunl)

at the larger chain of truck stops that had fast food outlets that were open and showers that were available. On the plus side, as a result of COVID-19, there is less traffic, no lineups and cheap fuel. Crossing back into Canada, Customs really doesn't ask me anything as they really don't want any communication with drivers and they have no desire to climb up into the truck to search it. Talking to some of my friends who were going across Canada, it was a different story. Food and showers were virtually non-existent. (Harry Bellam)

Sharing Canada's expertise

This crisis has seen unparalleled international cooperation. Canada has shared resources and expertise with other countries that are engaged in the common battle to eradicate COVID-19.

Dr. Bruce Aylward, renowned Canadian epidemiologist and Special Adviser to WHO's Director-General Dr. Tedros Adhanom Ghebreyesus, is a prime example. He directed the World Health Organization's evaluation of China's response to the initial outbreak in Wuhan province. In his report in late February, he commended China's actions and sounded a warning that time was of the essence in preparing other countries for the virus's spread there. Very soon afterwards, he led a mission to Spain to learn lessons from the rapid outbreak in that country to apply to other areas of the world.

Montrealer Gweneth Michelle Thirlwell, who works for Médecins Sans Frontières (Doctors Without Borders) in Montreal as a fundraiser and in the Field as an HR manager, is another Canadian who is supporting COVID-19 efforts in a foreign country. Her family has agreed to share some of their WhatsApp communications with her as she takes up this new challenge in Mexico. Gweneth's dad is an oncologist working at a hospital in Montreal that is engaged in COVID-19 testing.

> April 1 (Gweneth): Much of the world might be in lockdown mode but somehow I did the opposite today! I have started a 3-month mission in Mexico City to support MSF projects in Mexico as they prepare for and respond to COVID-19. Some trepidation over leaving home and my family in such uncertain times, but I feel honoured to be able to help others in need.
>
> April 15 (Gweneth) [her 2-week quarantine completed]: They are sending me to go help in a project on the border that needs HR help.
>
> April 15 (Dad): Remember, Stay Safe. Hand washing with soap ,where available and hand sanitizer, frequently after touching other things. No hands on the face. Follow the MSF personal protective instructions strictly. God bless. Love and prayers, Dad xo.
>
> April 16 (Gweneth): I arrived at the hub for the project: Reynosa. I was pulled aside at the airport and questioned about COVID symptoms while all the other passengers (Mexican) were allowed through, no problems. Apparently a state epidemiologist will call me this week to ensure I am asymptomatic. But honestly, everyone on that plane should be followed up on. I've just come out of quarantine. I am more safe than any other person on that flight! Security wise, things are OK here since there is nothing to do and no one is out and about. But the situation is always unpredictable due to the drug cartels in this part of Mexico.

April 21 (Gweneth): Hot and humid in Matamoros. Busy day. Lots of linguistic gymnastics switching between Spanish, French and English. Just taking a short break before doing a second round of work this evening. I haven't left the compound since Friday so I am being as safe as possible.

April 22 (Gweneth): Good Morning! Another hectic long day ahead. Hopefully just one week of this crazy schedule and then things will be in place and I can go back to a normal working day.

April 29 (Gweneth): There is a regular project here to provide mental health support and basic health care to migrants stuck at the border trying to get into USA . . . these people will have no access to health care if they get COVID. We are opening a 40 bed isolation center for mild and moderate cases. The local hospital only has 12 beds allocated for COVID . . . The migrants live in camp with no opportunity for isolation and no running water for hand washing. The situation in Tijuana on the border with California is much much worse. I am recruiting 100 people for 2 isolation centres of 40 beds each – medical staff, cleaning staff, and guards. . . we must also find providers to wash sheets and make food for patients.

May 4 (Gweneth): My first two weeks in Mexico City (CDMX -- Ciudad de México) were spent in quarantine in a lovely apartment with a rooftop terrasse. Within a week, I was told that I would stay in Matamoros until the end of my contract June 30. I have been in Matamoros two weeks now. It is 40 km from the Gulf of Mexico, on the border with Brownsville, Texas . . . the population is 500,000. Unfortunately, it is unsafe to walk around and go out to random places here as the drug cartels are strong and terrorize the migrants. While MSF is not targeted, there is always a risk of getting caught in the wrong place at the wrong time: a common theme on all MSF projects . . . We are setting up two 40-bed COVID

Gweneth Thirlwell setting up beds and oxygenators in Matamoros, Mexico (photo courtesy Gweneth Thirlwell)

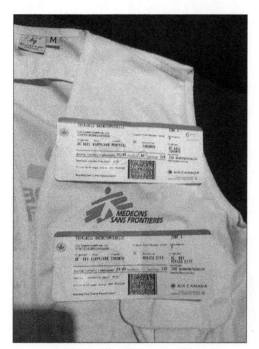

Gweneth Thirlwell's MSF vest and Mexico plane tickets (courtesy Gweneth Thirlwell)

isolation centres – one here in Matamoros and one in Reynosa. These are neighbouring border towns with a high number of migrants and individuals expelled from the USA. There are about 2000 people in a camp on the border in Matamoros and we are afraid that if COVID gets into the camp, it will spread like wildfire. Each family lives in a tiny tent right beside the next tent. Water and sanitation facilities are limited. They are right on a river but when COVID broke out, the authorities built a barbed wire fence around the camp cutting off access to the river where people used to bathe and wash their clothes . . .

My role in all of this is to recruit and hire 100 temporary employees: doctors, nurses, nurses aids, medical cleaners, orderlies, guards, drivers, and health promoters . . . The next two weeks will be the lead-up to an important turning-point for us. Matamoros is not seeing a sharp increase in COVID cases, and none in the migrant camp yet (knock-on-wood). So if this does not change in two weeks, we will consider shipping all of our supplies and teams to another location in Mexico where things are bad (i.e., Tijuana).

The office and living quarters are in a small gated-community of about 50 houses. MSF is renting 4 houses each with 3 bedrooms. They are North American style houses. Luckily with air conditioning for the days when the humidity is unbearable and the temperatures rise to 35 C. . . . The food is good ol' Mexican down-home cooking . . . the fruits and vegetable category gets covered off by the freshly-made tomato salsa and the fresh juices (mango, cucumber, papaya, watermelon, etc.) . . . In many ways I am still very much in North America . . . But in other ways, things are very much like being on a project in Africa: cold showers; limitations on movements due to danger from local fighting (in this case it is drug cartels); cultural and language barriers; and the slow-pace of things. Just when I get comfortable and think I am back in Canada, something happens to remind me that I am in an MSF project!

May 16 (Gweneth): Another grey, cool Saturday morning here, and it is even raining! . . . But again I don't get to stay cosy in bed. Team meeting at 8 a.m. to discuss the direction of the project in view of the lack of COVID explosion here. Then preparing 15 contracts for new starts on Monday. And then we get to assemble hospital-like beds for the COVID Centre. That will actually be the fun part except it will mean no nap today – not sure how Dad and Jean [my oldest sister who is a psychiatrist] have done it all these years: non-stop work without a full day of rest at any time.

Tributes

A huge THANK YOU! to all those working on the front lines, in whatever capacity, but especially those in the health care fields. (Jim Fraser and Carol Alette)

I would like to offer my most sincere condolences to all those who have suffered from COVID-19 and may have lost loved ones. (Lorenzo Tartamella)

I find myself crying when I learn of all those people in long-term care homes who have died all alone without their loved one by their side as they take their last breath. This is so very heart-wrenching. Mostly I am worried and sad. My hopes are that COVID-19 will end and that my family, friends and other people I know will remain safe and stay well. I pray for this. (Karen Jackson)

Our son, Scott, works for Starfish Medical in Vancouver – recently mentioned by Prime Minister Trudeau as one of the companies lined up to produce 30,000 ventilators. (Don and Glad Parsons)

Chapter 14
Partisan politics on pause

"Once upon a time" children's book cover
(credit: created by template.net)

Fifty or 100 years from now – when our grandchildren will have become grandparents themselves – the opening lines of a children's story book may read as follows:

> Once upon a time, a long time ago, in the year 2020, a great miracle happened. Politicians became people and worked together to defeat a mighty monster named COVID who was terrifying the land . . .

Of course, this is not a fairy tale – it actually happened. In a dramatic change of behaviour, our Canadian political leaders temporarily shed their partisan stripes to work as one to confront the challenges that faced them all.

In the weeks leading up to the coronaquake, it was "business as usual" in Canada's House of Commons where Members followed the long-established behaviour of their predecessors as partisan politicians. For years, the debates taking place in that august chamber had been characterized by rancour, heckling and name-calling – not to mention the insults, finger-pointing and one-upmanship – causing

Peace Tower, Parliament buildings, Ottawa
(photo by author)

the poor frustrated Speakers of the day to practically tear their hair out.

But all that was prior to March 13, when the House of Commons voted unanimously to suspend its sitting in the light of the COVID-19 crisis. The burning issues of the day (such as the First Nations railway blockades, western pipeline construction and the Iran air crash investigation) were put on the back burner in order to focus uniquely on the pandemic. For the following several weeks, cooperation replaced confrontation. Of course it was too good to last forever. Political partisanship did briefly return on March 24-25 during an emergency sitting to approve the first phase of the government's huge financial relief package. Opposition parties felt that the government was guilty of "overreach" and a "power grab," so they briefly blocked the legislation until an acceptable compromise was reached and unanimous consent was achieved.

During the ongoing crisis there was also remarkable cooperation between the federal and provincial governments as they coordinated their response, taking into account their respective jurisdictions and responsibilities.

American situation

South of the border, where partisan politics is perpetually at play, a somewhat similar situation was playing out but there were some important differences. In an environment of intense political polarization, the challenge of bringing about cooperation between the Republican and Democratic members of Congress was much more daunting. Memories of President Trump's impeachment trial and acquittal were still very fresh in everyone's minds.

An added factor was that the country was in full pre-election mode with elections slated for November. Nevertheless, there suddenly occurred a pause when

United States Capitol, Washington, D.C. (photo by author)

election fever was overtaken by a very different kind of fever. Even CNN, normally obsessed with politics, abruptly changed gears and rebranded itself as COVID Nineteen News. On March 27, the U.S. Senate unanimously approved a historic $2 trillion stimulus package. In terms of federal-state cooperation, there was considerably less cohesion than in Canada. In fact, in those states hardest hit by the virus, there was outright confrontation with the federal administration. In the meantime, the previously very animated race for the Democratic presidential nomination degenerated into a two-man contest and fizzled out entirely when Bernie Sanders threw in the towel on April 8.

Canada-U.S. relations

The fact that Canada and the United States are such close neighbours and such important trading partners is a significant factor in how the two countries are managing their joint response to the pandemic. Coming off the difficult but successful renegotiation of the Canada-US-Mexico Agreement (CUSMA), Canada had new challenges to face in the context of COVID-19. Critical among them was the delicate question of border closure. In addition, Canada successfully deflated President Trump's trial balloons regarding the stationing of troops on the Canada/ U.S.A. border and the redirection of personal protection equipment (PPE) destined for Canada. Playing a key role in these achievements was Deputy Prime Minister Chrystia Freeland, who had earned her stripes last year negotiating the new trade agreement.

Public faces of COVID-19

Throughout the early weeks of COVID-19, Canadians are receiving regular updates on the progress of the pandemic and the mitigation measures being taken. Among the plethora of politicians and medical professionals who deliver a daily diet of definitive directives and sobering statistics are the following now-familiar faces:

- Tedros Adhanom Ghebreyesus, Director-General of the World Health Organization (WHO)
- Justin Trudeau, Prime Minister
- Chrystia Freeland, Deputy Prime Minister
- François Legault, Quebec Premier
- Patty Hajdu, Minister of Health
- Dr. Theresa Tam, Chief Public Health Officer
- Dr. Horacio Arruda, Quebec Director of National Public Health

Each of them played leading roles in the daily drama that unfolded – on giant TV screens and on tiny smartphone displays alike – across the country from sea to sea to sea. It was indeed refreshing to see the softer sides of our politicians' personalities revealed, instead of the bluster and bravado to which some had occasionally been prone prior to the crisis.

Infections/death forecasts

Early on, we were told of the need to flatten or plank the curve but, as time went on, were given no indication of how effective all the

Public faces of COVID-19, top to bottom:
Tedros Adhanom Ghebreyesus, Justin Trudeau, Chrystia Freeland, François Legault, Patty Hajdu, Dr. Theresa Tam, Dr. Horacio Arruda
(TV screen shots by author and Elaine Fraser)

distancing rules were. There seemed to be a reluctance to reveal the results of forecasting models. Authorities indicated that they did not have sufficient quantity of quality data to prepare accurate projections. Perhaps the more likely reason for the delay in releasing the numbers was a concern about how the projections would be interpreted. On the one hand, if the projections were discouraging, people might despair and abandon the distancing guidelines. On the other hand, if the numbers were too favourable, people might become complacent and think that the battle had been won, hence there would be no more need for physical distancing. Either way, the release of this data would involve real risks.

In the end, vox populi ruled. On April 3, Premier Doug Ford announced Ontario's modelling projections and suddenly the floodgates opened. Provincial health experts said they expect COVID-19 could kill 3,000 to 15,000 people in Ontario over the course of the coronavirus pandemic, the ramifications of which could last up to two years.

Very soon afterwards, on April 7, Premier Legault released Quebec's modelling numbers that projected at least 1,263 COVID-19 deaths by end of April.

Finally, on April 9 the Public Health Agency of Canada released national modelling data with different possible scenarios, warning that what happens depends very much on how well Canadians respect the measures in place to keep the respiratory illness from spreading. In the worst-case scenario, where 70 to 80% of Canadians become infected, more than 300,000 would likely die. In the best case scenario, only 2.5 to 5% of Canadians would become infected and between 11,000 and 22,000 people would die.

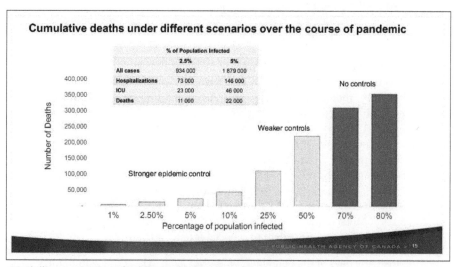

Modelling projections (Public Health Agency of Canada)

In mid-April there was a sharp increase in the number of deaths reported, especially among the elderly. Quebec's seniors' residences, including the CHSLDs (residential long-term care facilities) were extremely hard hit, causing Premier Legault to urgently appeal for additional resources from among the province's medical specialists and for the help of the Canadian Armed Forces medical corps. Among those who volunteered their services was Céline Leger, who had just returned from Senegal where she served as an operating room nurse with Mercy Ships. Céline writes:

> When I decided to offer my services I considered it to be a natural continuation of my humanitarian service, albeit at home instead of abroad. Upon arrival at the CHSLD, I was assigned as a nurse on the first floor. To begin with, I followed a nursing assistant who introduced me to the patients and explained their medications to me. That allowed me to learn their names and to understand their ability to respond. My job was to evaluate their overall condition including their sores, look after their bandages and perform other care tasks. A task that I really enjoyed was reviewing the residents' conditions with the doctor. This Centre's doctor really had a heart for her patients and was very proactive – so much so that I had to tell her "I will take care of it." At the end of a day, we were very proud of the work accomplished by our team. Most of the healthcare workers were new because so many of the original team had been afflicted with the virus at the outset of the pandemic. Joining me in responding to the government's urgent appeal were people from a wide variety of professions: archivist, doctor, hospital manager, daycare educator, nurses from other hospitals and newly graduated nurses; all dedicated to the same cause: to provide quality care. I salute them all.

> I would like to share the story of my encounter with one resident – an octogenarian who had tested positive for COVID-19 and was receiving palliative care. She was alone in her room and was quite unresponsive, although she was breathing quite well with a minimum of oxygen. But during the day her breathing became more difficult. As I looked at her, I thought of all the elderly who were alone without their families. I didn't know whether she could hear me or feel my presence. I gave her a final bit of care, then prepared to leave. But I couldn't leave. I looked at her again and tried to imagine being alone in her condition. So I went to her bedside, took her hand in mine and prayed together. I assured her that she was not alone, reminded her who she was and told her that she had never left that Great Source of Love who created her and would accompany her to return there. Be that as it may. I returned home but her face came back to me frequently, so I stopped and prayed for her again: "we are there for you, don't worry, the angels will welcome you . . ." Much to my surprise, we learned the next morning that she had passed away. I had a moment of silence for her.

In the early days of the pandemic, whenever I would hear the words "Mr. or Mrs. So-and-so died yesterday or last night" I would wonder how many died alone because of a lack of personnel, who were trying to cope as best they could. Let us hope that these souls did not pass on alone, but were escorted and welcomed. I lift my hat with much gratitude to all those who came to the rescue and together met the challenge to restore dignity to the elderly. For me, it was a return to my roots, because I began my nursing career working in a seniors' care centre. I loved my patients so much. It seems like yesterday. (Céline Léger)

In the United States Dr. Anthony Fauci, Director of the National Institute of Allergy and Infectious Diseases, predicted on March 30 that between 100,000 and 200,000 persons would die nationwide from the coronavirus.

Worldwide, as of May 19 there have been almost five million confirmed cases and more than 300,000 deaths. (source: World Health Organization, https:// COVID19.who.int/)

Comments about our leaders

Personally I feel that our country is in good hands with Mr. Trudeau's and Ms. Freeland's leadership. Here in Ontario, Premier Ford has proven to be an absolute rock! (Steve Fraser)

I listen to Prime Minister Trudeau's address to the nation every morning. I have become accustomed to the reports from other members of the government, from reporters and health care specialists and from provincial premiers. I am proud to be a Canadian and proud of how the country seems to be pulling together through all of this. (Diane Keet)

All levels of government have stepped up and taken timely action, relying on the advice of health professionals. Despite his wooden presentation style, I think that Premier Doug Ford is appropriately managing the challenges facing Ontario. At the federal level, Justin Trudeau and his ministers present quiet confidence, with a daily balanced message, not being afraid to announce bad news, but offering a realistic assessment of the future mixed with cautious optimism. Contrasting that to some of what we hear from elsewhere, all I can say is "Thank God we're in Canada!" (Frasier Bellam)

We listen religiously to the noon, 6 p.m. and 10 p.m. television news and to the daily updates of the Premier, the Health Minister and the Medical Director. We have nothing but praise for how our leaders have managed the crisis. (Jacques Crépeau and Ginette Arcand)

We are grateful to our governments who made us feel safe and compensated us with some funding as our finances become a challenge. (Lorenzo Tartamella)

Unfortunately, science has gone out of fashion in our current political climate here in the U.S. I'm an advocate for listening to the scientists (always) and the public health experts on this one. It's a biggie. Solve the public health crisis, and the healing of the economy will follow. There is a daily "briefing" on TV which is akin to a political rally, with unhinged political rantings and public health experts trying to thread the needle of believability. What exactly are the American people to believe? No, it is not a Democratic hoax. Yes, more could have been done sooner. But here we are, April 15, 2020, with over two million cases worldwide. (Sally Aldinger)

Our governments – federally, provincially, and municipalities as well – seems to be working more collaboratively now, as they try to find solutions to the problems we have never faced before. I can only hope that communication and non-partisan dialogue will continue in the future, both in our country and throughout the world. (Carol Alguire)

My cousin Ron Planche – himself a veteran political operative and politician – shares his views on politicians, policies and priorities in the context of the COVID-19 crisis:

There are three types of politicians – Liars, Lemmings and Leaders. Thank God we live in Canada and while I don't like our Premier in Ontario . . . I am quite impressed with his leadership and willingness to not practice demagoguery towards Ottawa. This is refreshing and has earned my respect.

Perhaps it is time to reimagine the role currently played by the military in our country and transition it to be an ultra-emergency response service provider during times of local or national crises. For example, in Quebec and other parts of Eastern Canada we had, several years back, that terrible ice storm. Most civil agencies were unable to cope and respond quickly. How would our country respond to a massive category 8 or 9 earthquake hitting Vancouver or a tsunami inundating a populated area of Vancouver or Nova Scotia? Even Ontario is at risk should a massive meltdown of one of our nuclear reactors occur. On the other hand, we cannot ensure that our First Nations communities get safe water, nor could we ensure that, if our own water supply was massively compromised, we could respond on a timely scale. The basic premise of a civil society is that its civil infrastructure works. When it does, our society is safe and secure. When it does not, all hell breaks loose! The current COVID-19 crisis shows how vulnerable we are when our instruments of infrastructure are unable to react – let alone be proactive. Enlightened political leadership can keep us safe, and a reimagined civil emergency response force can be a powerful tool in its arsenal. (Ron Planche)

As the COVID-19 crisis moves into a new phase, it is hoped that the laudable level of cooperation demonstrated by our leaders will continue.

Chapter 15
Technology to the rescue

"Technology" (istockphoto.com – credit Quardia)

Although I, like many, am technically challenged (my computer would still be running on DOS 1.0 were it not for my trusted technical trouble-shooter, Richard!), I have come to embrace technology and appreciate its enormous benefits. During this crisis, technology has come of age, as it were. No longer just enabling a playground for geeks with all its gizmos, gadgets and games, it has provided a veritable lifeline of services for many.

Above: Microsoft DOS 1.0 diskette (YouTube)
Right: Grandson Caleb's gaming cave (photo by Elaine Fraser)

The Internet

The Internet (istockphoto.com – credit Bet_Noire)

The Internet itself provides the backbone for practically all the other services. For me personally, in writing this book, its Google search engine has been indispensable in my research. By comparison, I think back to my first published document in 1964, "A Study of Winds and Blowing Snow in the Canadian Arctic," where my research was limited to sifting through dog-eared handwritten weather records in the dusty dingy archives in the catacombs of the Department of Transport's Adelaide Street building in Toronto.

Almost 25 years ago, when Internet was in its infancy, I wrote an Editorial "The Internet: Much more than a toy" in our family newsletter, the LINK, extolling the benefits of this new service. In revisiting it today, I am struck by how much of it still rings true:

> Until a couple of years ago, most of us had never heard of the Internet. Today, there are millions upon millions of people connected to it . . . Although its dramatic rise in popularity is very recent, the origins of the Internet date back more than 25 years. It was originally set up by the U.S. Defence Department as an interconnected series of mainframe computers located at major military installations, universities and defense contractors. It has grown into an intricately connected global network of millions of computers known as the World Wide Web. The Internet has made possible the exchange of information in a way never imagined a few short years ago. In terms of sheer volume, the amount of information available on the Internet is truly overwhelming. And, in

terms of content, it covers the whole spectrum, from the good to the bad to the very ugly. This is due to the fact that, until now, the content of websites has been almost totally uncontrolled. However, that problem now is being seriously addressed. Many people look at the Internet as entertainment – a sort of toy or game – something that is lots of fun but of little or no practical use. I cannot share that view. In the less than two years that I have been on the Internet, I have found it to be extremely useful. Here are a few of the many practical uses that we have seen.

- Travel: make an airline or hotel reservation
- Real estate: shop for a house
- Employment: browse job ads
- Courier services: schedule or track a delivery
- People finder: track down folks who have moved
- Medical: access tons of information on what ails you
- Shopping: buy anything and everything
- Homework: do research for school projects
- Environment: participate in environmental projects
- Religion: share one's faith

Providing that its darker side can be adequately controlled, the Internet will continue to grow in popularity and acceptance. I believe that it will soon become as indispensable a convenience of modern life for us as the telephone, the automobile and the flush toilet were to another generation. (Winston Fraser)

Online tools and services

While the Internet serves as the basis for online communications, there are many other components that facilitate the use of today's technology. Included among them are the following:

- web browsers (e.g., Google Chrome, Apple Safari, Firefox, Internet Explorer, Edge)
- online web applications (e.g., email, texting, social networking, videoconferencing, video sharing)
- mobile devices (e.g., smartphones, tablet PCs (iPads and others))
- mobile applications (also referred to as mobile apps or simply apps): computer programs or software applications designed to run on a mobile device
- communication protocols (e.g., https, Wi-Fi, Bluetooth, etc.)

Today everything can be interconnected – your camera to your TV, your doorbell to your smartphone, maybe even your dog's barking inhibitor device to your laptop!

Personal uses during COVID-19

Fraser Family Easter dinner on Zoom (screen shot by Jacob Lazda)

Several contributors to this book share how technology has helped them cope with the challenges of living under the laws of physical distancing:

> We have held weekly Tracy family gatherings on Zoom. These have been in the form of cocktail parties, updates, recipe-sharing and online games. Even my dad, at 90, is online with everyone each week. He says, with his ever-present wit, that we all "leave him speechless!" (Joanne Carruthers)

> Lately Carol and I have Skyped with various friends and family. While it's not the same as being with them in person, the visuals provide an extra level of emotional attachment. (Jim Fraser)

> I've seen friends on Zoom, which is better than not at all.   I'd never even heard of Zoom until mid-March. (Margaret Eastwood)

> I never would believe that I'd be praising technology. Yet today I give thanks for the ease by which we remain connected. Church services, dance parties, meetings, happy hours and just visual chats. (Betty Maine, excerpted from a story in Chapter 18)

> Our main contact with our children – one in Sofia and the other in Hong Kong – is via WhatsApp, certainly a marvellous way to keep in touch over long distances. We've been in video contact more often since COVID-19 using FaceTime for one of our children because we have a new iPad. And with all four of us together, it's been with Hangouts. Margaret has watched some virtual church services, such as for Easter Sunday. (David and Margaret Gussow)

It is possible to stay connected without being physically present. We have Zoom cocktails with our ski instructor friends every Saturday at 4 p.m. – the same time we would typically gather at the local pub after a day of teaching. We have Zoom dinners with Liam, Karri, Delaney, Luke, and Sean's sister, Maureen, at least once a week. The Tracy family has been having calls every Sunday to check in – lately they have included trivia games and challenges. Last week we had calls with friends in Ottawa (Friday cocktails for them) and Australia (Saturday morning coffee). A professional association with which I am involved has regular networking calls called "I Love this Bar." (Pat Tracy-Callahan)

We, myself included, are learning new ways of communicating through digital channels, like FaceTime, WhatsApp, Zoom and others. Will this be maintained forever instead of personal interaction at group and family gatherings? I hope not totally. (Carol Alguire)

We've done Zoom chats with the whole family the last three weeks. (Jennifer Tracy)

My granddaughter Arabella's 4th birthday was celebrated without Gramma and family and friends. I did, however, with the help of technology, have a video chat and was able to join in the singing of Happy Birthday and watch her blow out the candles. That made me grateful and thankful for this technology. (Karen Jackson)

The technological learning curve has been quite steep, but there is definitely an advantage to having such a short commute! (Andrea Fraser)

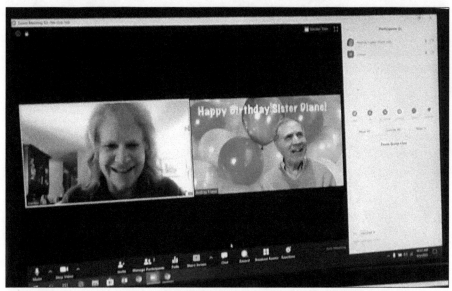

Zoom birthday chat with my baby sister (screen shot by Andrea Fraser)

My brother Malcolm (Moose) died on March 16 after a lengthy and devastating illness, not related to COVID-19. With the pandemic, it was not possible to physically get together with family, friends and community members to share our grief and memories. So, thanks to Zoom, an online funeral/memorial service was arranged and held on March 29. It provided some much-needed closure until such time as we all can physically gather together to remember Moose. It was a moving service, and my heart felt so much lighter afterwards. (Diane Keet)

We use Zoom to stay in touch with our large family (we have six children) who so far are all doing well. (Bob Simon)

Screen shot of online Zoom family funeral (photo by Elaine Fraser)

Something is still missing

In spite of the wonders of today's technology, there is still something missing in the absence of direct human contact. My parish priest shares how COVID-19 and the rules of physical distancing have affected her:

> Over the past several weeks, it seems like the whole world has turned upside down. Fear of contagion has completely changed the ways in which we interact. For me, it is not fear of contracting COVID-19 – I am not particularly vulnerable to a more serious expression of the disease – but it is fear of passing it on to someone who is. This means I take very seriously the public health advice to avoid any but the most essential "in person" interactions. There is very little that I consider essential: I go to the grocery store about once every 10 days and I have been to the pharmacy once; I visit two empty churches to make sure there is no damage to our unused buildings; I walk my dog, making sure I keep a

good distance from anyone else on the forest paths. This does not mean I am not busy and am not working.

Technology has allowed me to continue working, except that all contact is digital. This technology has been a blessing, but has also been frustrating and has proved to have a steep learning curve. I keep thinking that next week will slow down, next week I will start getting bored. It has slowed down to a certain extent, but the low-level anxiety due to the state of the world has meant that most things take more energy than they would in happier and healthier times. It is difficult to digest all of the bad news we hear from our (more or less) trusted news sources, especially when human companionship is limited. There is only so much connection to be had over a Zoom call.

This time of social isolation has highlighted the effects of living on my own. There is no one in my family I can see in person or touch. There is no one at my dining table other than the dog at my feet who is still waiting for scraps. I don't know what this lack of human interaction will mean in the long run but, for the present, I know that living on my own has had repercussions that I did not expect and that I do not think are healthy for the body or mind. We live in a world that values independence and self-actualization, but this period of self-isolation is underlining the importance of connection and inter-dependence. I hope that this time will teach me to see and nurture what is most valuable in my life so that when we can be together again in person, we will live into the truly essential "in person" interactions that give meaning to our lives. (Rev. Sophie Rolland)

Chapter 16
Isolation living

Playing Scrabble with my granddaughter Micayla (photo by
Elaine Fraser)

At first, the prospect of self-isolation for an indefinite period of time seemed very
daunting – a scary sentence of unending solitary confinement separated from our
loved ones. However, once resigned to our fate, many of us have succeeded in
making the best of it.

This chapter documents some of the activities in which people have engaged that
have allowed them to not only survive isolation and avoid going stir crazy, but to
experience some very positive aspects in the process. Perhaps others' activities
documented below will serve as an inspiration – or even a challenge – to the
reader.

Personal relationships

*"A person is a person through other persons; you can't be human in isolation; you
are human only in relationships."* (Desmond Tutu)

Self-isolation provides endless opportunities for both togetherness and aloneness.
People share the pros and cons of each:

We are getting to know people differently. On a recent staff call, one of the environmental managers noted that we are seeing a different side of our co-workers. We are now in their homes, meeting their pets and children, seeing the insides of their bedrooms, garages, kitchens, and basements. Nobody apologizes for noisy children or barking dogs. One co-worker noted that he has had to remember to make his bed every day! (Pat Tracy-Callahan)

As a family, within days we found the strength to remain spiritually grateful and calendar-ready, where Sunday still feels like a Sunday and Friday nights became movie night for us. Our relationships grew stronger, and the understanding of each other as modern teens improved. We do worry about the future but live these treasured moments because they will someday end. Our lives and the freedom to enjoy travelling, sports arenas, and more may have stopped, but having each member of the family make their own adjustments is like one of the best vacations ever, or, as my son calls it, a coronacation. This tragic pandemic has helped us achieve some of the peace we needed. (Lorenzo Tartamella)

I am grateful my two older daughters share an apartment in Montreal so that they can care for each other. My son has had ample time to spend with his new girlfriend because her job got cancelled, so they've been building a solid friendship. My older three remember the ice storm of '98 with fond memories of loads of playtime. I hope our memories of this season of our lives will be mostly positive. Tensions in our couple and with our resident senior have become more pronounced. (Jennifer Tracy)

The most difficult part of "self-isolating" is not being able to get together and share a meal and an evening with our family and friends. This is such a regular and valued part of our routine that we have made great efforts to gather together weekly for "virtual game nights" on the weekends. Although it is definitely not the same as being together in person, it is still fun and great to stay connected this way. As I am writing this, I am thinking about how to decorate the kitchen for our Zoom Easter dinner with the kids tomorrow. (Andrea Fraser)

During this time I've had a lot more time to reflect and think about what things mean to me. Our normal used to consist of driving our kids (ages 11, 9, 7, 5) to and from activity after activity – barely having enough time to have a meal together, let alone get to know each other. The kids would get off the bus and I would shove a bit of food into their mouths and then we would hop in the car to go to the next activity. They (the kids) didn't talk to one another – nor did they seem to get along. Fast forward to March break (March 15, 2020). After the first few days in isolation at home, our 9-year-old says "I kind of like not being so busy – we get more time to play." For the first time in years, my children were getting along. They were listening to each other, making up games and just playing like kids do. Over the weeks, their bonds/friendships have strengthened to a degree I never thought imaginable. The two oldest

Sisters Skyleigh and Soleil having fun (photo by Jennifer Hurd)

girls are requesting sleepovers in each other's rooms, hanging out and talking to each other like friends. My hope for them is that, no matter what happens in this world, they remember that family is so important – we always come back to our roots! (Jennifer Hurd)

It's sad that there is a pandemic but, in a way, I am okay with what it has forced us to do. Obviously I miss my friends and extended family, like my grandparents, that I cannot see, but I am enjoying the online school and hanging out with my siblings more. Before this happened, school was so rushed. We might only have 30 minutes a day to work on a project but at home I have as much time as I need. Also, when I got off the bus, I was always heading to something else straight from school. Now it is all online and I am not going place to place. My dance is online. I miss being at the dance studio and seeing my dance friends and teacher, but the online classes help a lot with my technique and I also get to work with other dance teachers from all over the world! Some things we do to keep ourselves busy are go for walks, play outside, build forts, do baking and even have sleepovers with our siblings in each other's rooms. Even though I am okay with what this has forced us to do, I do hope that our world, my family and friends will all make it out safely on the other side. (Skyleigh Hurd, age 11)

The absolute worst to come out of this isolation is not being able to see Mom. It is something I try not to focus on. It breaks my heart that Mom and Dad have to be apart after they've been together every day. Nursing homes seem to be places where the virus likes to settle and spread. I read the news every day, terrified that her facility will be named. (Kerri Fraser)

This pandemic has changed my life personally this past month. With George in a long-term care facility, I have been unable to visit him. Furthermore, I have not seen the personal support workers, nurses and residents of Rosebridge, all of whom I have grown to know and love. This has saddened me so very much. However, I do understand the importance of physical distancing. On the plus side, George phones me almost daily, so we do stay connected. Easter has come and Easter has gone – celebrating it alone. But I did prepare a meal of fried ham, fried eggs and mashed potatoes just like we used to do at Pine Hill Farm and I reminisced – lots of time for this. (Karen Jackson)

We have a lot more written, verbal and video conversations with children, grandchildren, brothers, sisters, other relatives, friends and the priest. I've been living at the same address for more than 20 years and I can count on my fingers the number of times that my neighbour has spoken to me. However, since COVID-19, we speak much more often. He tells me about his hunting adventures and gave me a book about venison and how to cook it. (Jacques Crépeau and Ginette Arcand)

The COVID-19 pandemic turned our lives upside down in only a matter of days. Daniel had been working at a potash mine about three hours away from home. He is gone all week and comes home on the weekends. Four days after the COVID chaos began in Saskatchewan, Daniel was sent home from work for two weeks of isolation because his co-worker/ roommate had earlier gone to Mexico. Although neither Daniel nor his roommate had symptoms, they were sent home as a precaution. During those two weeks, it was discovered that Daniel's other roommate/co-worker had been to a snowmobile rally and banquet at Christopher Lake (Saskatchewan) on March 14 where 18 new cases of COVID-19 had been identified. Therefore Daniel's isolation continued longer than anticipated. Fortunately neither he nor his roommates contracted the virus. (Tara Abramyk)

I am making more personal contact with people now by phone, rather than emailing, in order to have a friendly conversation and hear the other person's voice. This is a positive outcome. (Carol Alguire)

Reading, writing and a rhythm shtick

Many folks pass their confinement hours exercising the original 3 R's of learning – reading a good book, writing some prose or poetry, or adding to their musical repertoire. Personally, since I am not a reader and because I am void of any musical talent, I have opted for the second R. An old IBM colleague has chosen the first R:

I'm relying on my library and the Internet for useful pastimes. I'm quite enjoying the solitude. Reading books and surfing the net. Fortunately, I still get my daughter's gift (Sunday New York Times) delivered each week. If this "thing" lasts for months or years, I'll finally have the incentive to read everything on my shelves. By the way, I've noticed that all those spam telephone calls have ceased. (George Dunbar)

One of my high school classmates at Cookshire High School, Montreal singer and songwriter Jim Robinson, composed the following very topical song during his isolation:

LOTS OF TIME
by Jim Robinson

ever get the feeling i can't do this anymore
i've been told to isolate today is just day four
we've had other viruses but never one like this
the others came pretty close this one doesn't miss

it's on the news it's all the talk it's taken over the world
i try to push the news aside but when i give that a whirl
I think i may be missin' out so i turn the radio on
the hand wipes have disappeared and the toilet paper is gone

give me hope give me spring
give me a bit of everything
give me a thread throw me a line
no hurry i've got lots of time

they've shut schools and churches, restaurants 'n stores
no more concerts no more shows no more bars 'n no more sports
no more touchin' no more kissin' or even standin' close
you come any nearer and i'll punch you in the nose

give me hope give me spring
give me a bit of everything
give me a thread throw me a line
no hurry i've got lots of time

so it's wash your hands for 20 seconds don't touch your face
give everyone you encounter six feet of space
sneeze and cough into your elbow, believe me that's a test
go to supermarkets and drugstores give everything else a rest

give me hope give me spring
give me a bit of everything
give me a thread throw me a line
no hurry i've got lots of time

no one knows just when or how this is gonna end
in the meantime it's a good time to reach out to old friends
learn a new language write a book the one that's overdue
take up sewing or painting just don't get this bloody flu

give me hope give me spring
give me a bit of everything
give me a thread throw me a line
no hurry i've got lots of time

Jim's partner, Susan Fowler, keeps busy with a variety of creative endeavours, including her "The BEAR NEWS" newsletter that she has produced for several years. Recent issues have included COVID-19 topics. Her stated objective is to make people laugh and to express gratitude for the sometimes overlooked present-moment surprises and pleasures of all our daily lives.

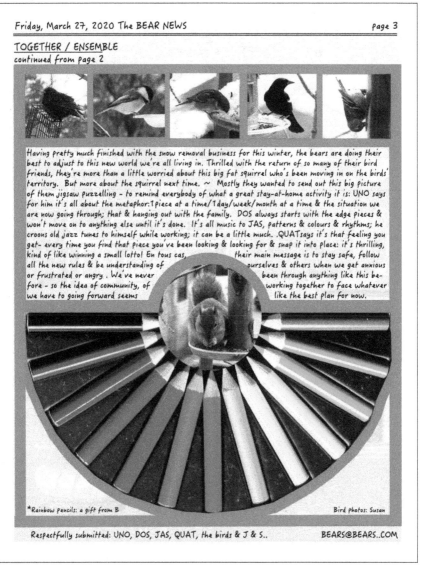

The BEAR NEWS newsletter, March 27, 2020 (courtesy Susan Fowler)

A friend of my brother Steve contributed this poem she felt inspired to write in the midst of the COVID-19 pandemic:

The power of compassion
by Niki Underhill

The world is changing
And so are we
Friends and family
Human kind
Collectively
To accept
Our new normality
A reality
With fewer smiles
And less hugs
With distant neighbors
That fear touch
But connection continues
Through screens and windows
Where hearts still glow
In all who know
That love is infectious
And time is extended

A time to grow
Exposed
To the errors of old
So we can create new
And release
The tendency to do
Instead
We can just be
Grateful for those
Who put food on our tables
And nurse us to health
Our greatest wealth
When we are not able
For all impacted
A call to action
Let us stand united
And when the truth
Is hard to fathom
Observe
The power of compassion

Music is used to brighten a shut-in's day, as illustrated in the following touching story from my cousin Charles:

> Because I can no longer visit her in person, every day I call my wife Myrna (who is an advanced Alzheimer resident in a care facility) and I sing to her over the telephone. Although she is no longer able to speak, the nurses tell me that she smiles when I sing, so that makes me feel happy. (Charles W.K. Fraser)

Reaching out and reconnecting

It's given me the opportunity to reconnect with some friends with whom I hadn't been in touch for quite some time. I had a Skype date with my best friend, Heather, in Montreal and her two kids who are around the same age as my boys. Unfortunately, due to distance, we haven't had the luxury of playdates and having our kids get to really know each other. The kids had a blast showing each other their toys via video chat. (Tara Abramyk)

Like everywhere, we see signs of creativity and ways that people are reaching out to others. On the covered bridge leading into our village, someone placed a teddy bear with a sign advising social distancing and saying, "Together we will get through this." Tacked to the bridge railings were individual bags of candy with notes on the outside saying, "Have a sweet walk, Love Social Distancing." (Pat Tracy-Callahan)

I have talked to friends on the phone that I hadn't been in touch with for a very long time, which is a good thing. (Margaret Eastwood)

Arranging and sorting

COVID-19 has given us lots of time indoors. I'm spending countless hours reviewing, tweaking and tagging some of my tens of thousands of photos, as well as commencing to sort through some of the many boxes of papers I brought home from my employment at Nortel and ST Microelectronics. The end (of either task) is nowhere near in sight! (Jim Fraser)

Richard and I have used some of our time to put together our photo albums from our Fraser Tour of Scotland in 2018. It has been so wonderful to live that trip all over again. We are now organizing our photos from our extended trip with Jimmy and Carol following the tour. Next will be our Danube River cruise from last June. Eventually, maybe I will have time to organize the pictures from all my student trips to Europe. (Diane Keet)

When I just can't sit at the computer any longer, I start working on cleaning projects that I never make the time to do. If there is something urgent for work that needs attending to, I go "back to the office" to take care of it, then continue cleaning. Although I know I won't get all the projects done, I will certainly have accomplished way more than I normally would have. (Andrea Fraser)

I seem to keep busy in isolation doing who knows what, but I've managed to avoid housework so far. Our small town (Niagara-on-the-Lake, Ontario) is under a state of emergency until at least June 30 because, being a huge tourist destination near the U.S. border, the Lord Mayor wants to keep us isolated as long as possible. We may finally emerge as a group of antisocial people with long hair, permanently dressed in PJ's! (Sally Harmer)

Now that I can't go visit my wife at the Home, I spend most of my time cleaning up areas that I've never had time to do because I was always too busy. (Charles W.K. Fraser)

Spring cleanup

We are coping quite well, happy to be in our own home and living in the country during these uncertain times. Being on our own property with neighbours near but not too close, we can be outside working around the grounds. Tasks include spring clean-up in the small barnyard; checking the fence around the pasture for our horse, Gypsy; raking the remains of winter twigs, small stones, etc. from the lawns; cleaning off the flower beds; and looking at the vegetable garden area with hope of being able to plant our usual seeds and plants for the coming season. (Sharon Moore and Royce Rand)

Our yard has been raked. The city compost cycle is still on the once-a-month winter schedule. But we've had a mild spring and lots of time for yard work, so all five of our bins are full and waiting to be emptied and refilled. (Jennifer Tracy)

We are keeping busy with the normal spring work: repairing the chicken coop, putting the hens outdoors and fixing the roof gutters while Ginette cleans up the grounds. (Jacques Crépeau and Ginette Arcand)

James and Tania have their girls helping with cleaning, picking up sticks and stones from the lawn and cleaning the garage. By the time this is all over, they will certainly know what "ménage" is. (June Patterson)

Physical exercise

We are all concerned about the current situation and the potential impact of COVID-19, and I wanted to remind everyone that we should still continue to exercise regularly. Unfortunately, during these times of crisis, our physical activity is often one of the first aspects of our lives we tend to ignore. We must try to avoid this. Being more physically active will not only help maintain our current physical and mental health – it can also help us prevent other diseases and conditions. (Aaron Fellows, Project Coordinator anr Kinesiology Clinic Supervisor, Department of Kinesiology and Physical Education, McGill University)

I have been able to develop a morning routine that includes both yoga and an hour-long walk on the trails before work. (Andrea Fraser)

Taking long walks along the Lakeshore has been a peaceful time for me – the water, the waves . . . so soothing. (Elaine Fraser)

My neighbour and I walk our dogs in the middle of side streets every evening. I have never walked so much in my life (15,000 steps a day!). (Margaret Eastwood)

Lauryn and I have been trying our best to get outside at least once per day and doing small forms of exercise. We are lucky to have Mt. Royal right behind us to allow us to get some fresh air as well as pleasant views of the city/forests. We look forward to being able to go back to Saint-Lazare to see Nessie (our dog) and go camping in our backyard if we have to! (Mattias Lazda)

I go outside every day and take a walk to the pond or in the field. I feel so fortunate to live here in the country. (June Patterson)

We typically take a walk twice a day, along the Rideau River across from our home and/or through our neighbourhood, of course always maintaining physical distancing from others – which still feels strange and unfriendly. (Jim Fraser)

Our daily exercise program was at the community centre for aerobics, weights, etc. Now we take walks for at least an hour, exploring different areas in our neighbourhood. Also, there is a YouTube video that gives us most of the same exercise moves that we had in the community centre. We use Chromecast to put it on the basement TV and follow it for about a half hour every day. (David and Margaret Gussow)

I had been lifting some old rusty weights in my basement when I opened your email about the book. I'm doing this only because my local gym, Goodlife, is closed. I had bought a set of Weider weights as a scrawny kid in Grade 9 to build up my physique. They are the originals with metal plates and wrench-on collars to hold them – two dumbbells and a long bar; very noisy and clumsy every time you change plates. I think it was a 110 lb. set that the high school offered for $25. I didn't know why I kept them all these years – but now I do! (Bruce Singleton)

Sean and I go for walks every day – some days on the roads and others through the woods along the cross-country ski trails. It's eerie as we walk by inns and restaurants that are empty. To avoid other walkers, we cross and walk in the middle of the road because there are so few cars in the village. (Pat Tracy-Callahan)

Since the beginning of the pandemic, almost every day until April 1, I have gone cross-country skiing in the soybean fields behind my house. I'd really like to swap my skis for my bike, but since cycling involves a greater risk of falling, I prefer to wait until things get back to normal. I don't want to end up in hospital during the pandemic. We regularly take walks of several kilometres on the streets of the municipality. (Jacques Crépeau and Ginette Arcand)

Royce does his own form of exercising: raking the lawns, checking the pasture fences and clearing debris from the small brook, as well as clearing fallen branches, cutting them up and stacking them to dry for firewood come the winter months. My sports and recreation is going for 40-45 minute walks along the quieter roads near our home. However, I am not committed enough to be out "no matter what the weather" but during those times I practise some of the exercises taught at the Senior's Fitness Exercise program that began in September 2019 at Grace Village (Huntingville). (Sharon Moore Rand)

Stay away from those addictive "screens" and get outside for some fresh air with your son. Maybe he'd love to play catch with Dad. That would be good for both of you. (George Dunbar)

During my emergency isolation in Dorval, I noticed that my grandchildren were digging out old toys and equipment that hadn't seen the light of day for many years, such as roller blades and a scooter. (Winston Fraser)

My grandkids out for a skate and a scoot (photo by author)

Family assembling giant jigsaw puzzle
(courtesy Carol Rand)

Fun and games

We spend a lot more time playing board games and cards together. (Tracie Dougherty)

One day James [my grandson] took the girls for a drive into the country and played the game "Get Daddy Lost." At each intersection, the girls took turns telling him which way they should turn – left or right. After driving in this manner for a total of 79 km, they suddenly shouted "There is Granny's house!" After all the random turns, they ended up coming down our back road – only five minutes away from where they started! (June Patterson)

We are reading more and have tried Netflix. (Art Pease)

I was joking that isolation/social distancing hasn't really impacted me, as most of my friends are 1300 km away in Nova Scotia and I normally only connect with them by phone anyways. Kennedy came up with a fun event on a Friday night that required all of us to secretly come up with a costume impersonating a celebrity – "Celebrities at supper." We are now sharing making supper amongst the four of us – it can be anything, and the rules are that everyone is supportive and approaches it with an open mind. We have news-free Friday evenings where we grab a beverage and all participate in completing the crossword from the Globe and Mail, hilariously moderated by Kennedy. And I grew a COVID-19 beard. (Charles C. Fraser)

"Celebrities at supper:" Duck Dynasty, Stevie Nicks, Hailey Baldwin Bieber, Diane Keaton

Having retired at the end of December 2014, I had a more-or-less fixed daily and weekly routine. I played tennis three times a week and social Bridge on Wednesday afternoons. But then, on March 15, all that stopped. Despite the frustration of the cancellation of the above activities, I feel very lucky to be retired, in relatively good health, financially secure, and living in my own home. I now fill my time with Internet Bridge, playing cribbage with my brother, crossword puzzles, TV, emailing friends and family, and taking walks around the neighborhood. My former employer contacts me occasionally to do some trouble-shooting, or to tweak some software that I had written way-back-when to meet new business requirements. (Frasier Bellam)

My two grandsons, Brody and Aiden, aged 11 and 12, decided one day to create surgical masks. Using folded paper towel and an elastic band, they made two prototypes that they judged to work well. When their mother asked how they knew, Brody replied "I breathed through it onto my hand, and couldn't feel my breath!" (Carol Rand)

Despite the restrictions in place, I was able to celebrate my grandson Lowell's 18th birthday. Being unable to go out to buy a gift, I decorated a box by stitching old metal work buttons on all sides and put some money inside. Then I delivered it to his family's front doorstep and expressed good wishes from a safe distance when they opened the door to retrieve it. (Carol Rand)

We have started to have campfires in the evenings. (Jacques Crépeau and Ginette Arcand)

Carol Rand's grandsons Brody and Aiden test their home-made masks (photo courtesy Carol Rand)

We do crossword puzzles and Sudoku, read The Record, magazines and books, and watch television programs. (Sharon Moore and Royce Rand)

I engaged in a variety of activities and actions during my first three weeks of isolation. In Week 1, I furiously cleaned out closets, preparing dozens of bins for various charities including my local hospital. For them, I packaged up all but a few of my precious N95 masks, gloves and other personal protective equipment to aid in the extreme shortages. In Week 2, with more time on my hands, I wrote more blog entries and signed up for Netflix. Zoom facilitated a Rotary meeting, our apartment

Carol Rand's home-made birthday gift for grandson (photo by Carol Rand)

complex's happy hour and a meeting of single friends. This virtual life was a breeze. At the dawning of Week 3, my usual sunny outlook was absent. I wasn't lonely or depressed, so what was going on? A Harvard Business Review article put a name to it: I was feeling the collective world grief as we struggled not to panic with the fear of the unknown. As prepared as I was in all aspects of the physical challenges, I didn't count on this grappling with grief. I sought the counsel of a few friends, prayed, and gave myself the time to bounce back. That is where I am now. The near future plan? I will continue to write, stay in touch, limit the TV news to programs that are helpful without extreme negativity. I'll go to church virtually, I'll watch The Crown and read books. Maybe I'll let Keith Urban teach me the guitar that I bought two years ago with his instructional DVDs. I have done all I need to do from a planning and cleaning perspective to shelter in place, safe from the boogieman COVID-19. Now I have to just let go and do those things I never had enough time to do. (Betty Maine)

I started and stopped working on assembling a large puzzle after realizing that I prefer puzzles as a social activity – a few friends, a glass of wine, and picking away at a puzzle as we chat. Sean and I unapologetically binge-watch Netflix. (Pat Tracy-Callahan)

As for my own isolation experience, it is a tale of two cities. I began my confinement at my eldest daughter's home in Saint-Lazare, a bedroom community about an hour west of Montreal. Then, as mentioned in Chapter 2, I moved to my second daughter's home in the Dorval suburb of Montreal for two weeks before returning to my original isolation hideout. In addition to being glued to my comfy swivel office chair penning the pages of this book, I take a daily rain-snow-or-shine walk in nearby woods with my faithful and fur-full collie, Prince. I have also enjoyed playing two very vintage games that were uncovered during my daughter's cleanup binges in the basement and in the garage – crokinole and croquet. So I'm keeping busy, staying fit and having fun. What more could I ask for?

My daily walk with Prince (photo by Andrea Fraser)

Playing crokinole (photo by Andrea Fraser)

On a lighter note

The following snippets are offered to support the old saying that "Laughter is the best medicine."

On the one-lane covered bridge in Jackson, N.H., cars have always had to yield, but now, with physical distancing, it is the pedestrians who must wait on one side until the others have crossed! (Pat Tracy-Callahan)

Covered bridge, Jackson, N.H. (Pat Tracy-Callahan)

An email that is making the rounds on the Internet adds a bit of levity to the rules under which we are currently living. Here are a few excerpts:

- I need to practice social-distancing from the refrigerator.
- Still haven't decided where to go for Easter: The Living Room or The Bedroom
- My body has absorbed so much soap and disinfectant lately that when I pee it cleans the toilet.
- Day 6 of homeschooling: My child just said "I hope I don't have the same teacher next year."
- Better six feet apart than six feet under. . .

My cousin Art Pease sent me the illustration opposite of physical distancing down on the farm.

A former colleague forwarded me a most hilarious video clip showing how a young couple countered the boredom of isolation life by simulating, inside their home, a man riding a horse. A screen shot of the horse galloping with its curly blonde tail flying is reproduced on the following page.

Finally, there is a clever piece of unknown origin that my niece-in-law, Jennifer Tracy, recently brought to my attention:

A Vermonter's guide to physical distancing (courtesy Art Pease)

Everyone needs to be careful because people are going crazy from being in isolation! Actually, I've just been talking about this with the microwave and toaster while drinking coffee and we all agreed that things are getting bad. I didn't mention anything to the washing machine as she puts a different spin on everything. Certainly not to the fridge as he is acting cold and distant. The vacuum was very unsympathetic . . . told me to just suck it up, but the fan was more optimistic and hoped it would all soon blow over!

Meanwhile, the blender has mixed feelings and the taps kept running hot and cold about the idea. The whisk refused to talk about it because she didn't want to whip things into a frenzy and the eggs kept quiet because they didn't want to get a beating. I didn't check with the oven because she's far too hot headed. The garbage bin just spouted a whole load of rubbish about the situation and the freezer gave me a frosty reception. The tin without a label, at the back of the cupboard, thinks it's a total mystery.

The knife made some very cutting remarks. The squash was very cordial about it all. Unlike the lemon who was very bitter about it. The toilet looked a bit flushed when I asked its opinion and didn't say anything, but the door knob told me to get a grip. Finally the front door said I was unhinged and so the curtains told me to – yes, you guessed it – pull myself together! In the end, the iron straightened me out as she said everything will be fine; no situation is too pressing. (author unknown)

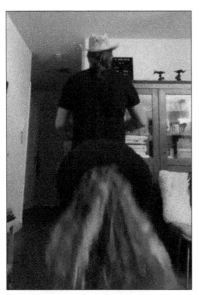

"Giddy-up!" (courtesy Larry Diamond)

Corona ball (courtesy Pat Tracy-Callahan)

Chapter 17
Emotions of many colours

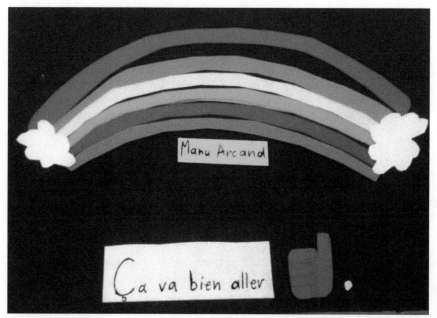

Rainbow drawing "Ça va bien aller" by 9-year-old Manu Arcand (photo by Daniel Arcand)

The Oxford Dictionary defines emotion as "a strong feeling deriving from one's circumstances, mood, or relationships with others." In the context of the current circumstances of the COVID-19 pandemic in general and isolation in particular, many different emotions are experienced, both positive and negative. Examples of positive feelings include love, hope, gratitude, admiration, pride and inspiration. On the more negative side are such emotions as anxiety, fear, sadness, grief, frustration and depression. In this chapter, contributors share the feelings that they have experienced. In addition, strategies are offered for the maintenance of one's mental wellness during the pandemic.

Positive feelings

I minimize my exposure to news articles and social media stories of death tolls, etc. Instead I focus on being productive in and around my home, my family, my work and on the beauty of the outdoors and the signs of spring. (Elaine Fraser)

I have no fears, because I believe the Holy Spirit will guide me day by day, no matter what happens. I have hope for the future, because I believe this crisis will redirect our paths, both personally and collectively as a nation. Hopefully this pandemic will help the global population to finally realize that we are all ONE in God's world, and to learn to love one another, following "the way, the truth, and the life." (Carol Alguire)

As we look around, we must dwell on the positive, being thankful for our own situation and reaching out with love and support to those who are suffering from health issues, loneliness and fear. We go for a 50-minute walk up McDonald Road each day, order groceries online and have them delivered to our driveway. We have good neighbours across the street that check on us and often run errands for us. We also spend considerable time on the phone or by email checking on each other – relatives, neighbours, friends and acquaintances. (Don and Glad Parsons)

Roller coaster at La Ronde, Montreal (photo by author)

So you go through a roller coaster of ups and downs. Of staying positive, making the most of your time reading, walking, maybe doing some much-needed organizing. You fear for those you care about, especially the elderly like my parents. For the most part what keeps me sane is the thought that this has to end. Praise God that, at the time of writing this from isolation, all is well and all precautions are being taken here. (Lisa Taubensee)

I hope and pray that we will all get through this together, even though we are apart for now. (Diane Keet)

We hope that it doesn't last too long. We want to get back to travelling. (David and Margaret Gussow)

We hope that certain habits acquired during isolation will remain after the pandemic. We hope that buying local – buying Quebec and Canadian products – will increase. We hope that we will soon be able to restore personal contact with our loved ones. (Jacques Crépeau and Ginette Arcand)

After a busy day, I appreciate being able to witness the calm and Zen that our beautiful planet faithfully provides in spite of the "crazy" that we all face. (Elaine Fraser)

A peaceful moment by Lac Saint-Louis (photo by Micayla Beck)

I feel grateful for each new day, for my family and community. I am fortunate to have my retirement check and to own my home free and clear, although I realize many others are not so fortunate. There is food (and TP!) in our storeroom. My satellites are working for TV and Internet. There is still water flowing in the creek, and stars and planets are in the sky. School is closed, but the school bus comes out our road each day to deliver lunches, work packets and library books. My daughter, Sarah, who unfortunately has lost a great deal of her income as an event planner due to the virus, goes to town for the mail and is also helping a few other elders who are staying home, including a 90-year-old neighbor. And we've all learned to Zoom! What is not zooming is the pace of life. As people rush to return to "normal," I hope we all remember that there was also beauty in this time, a certain peacefulness and time for reflection, as well as permission to just do a little bit of nothing sometimes. (Sally Aldinger)

I am so grateful to be retired from my work at the airport. It has become a scary place. My husband Rick is grateful to be retired from managing a seniors' home, since that is a hot spot for this disease. I'm grateful for Netflix. I have increased gratitude for simple things like delivery trucks, the freedom to shop, a smile from a stranger and health. (Jennifer Tracy)

First, I am thankful for what I have – that I live a very simple life and live in the country with land to move and work on. I am thankful for my family, with whom we are in contact every day, and that they are safe and healthy as I am writing this. I am thankful for my friends with whom we are in frequent contact. (Barb Ward)

179

I am so thankful that I live "in nature" and that one of the activities I love most is just being outdoors. I am thankful to have this time to enjoy experiencing spring as it unfolds into summer. Although the self-isolation is cramping my "wanderlust" style right now, I know that eventually the restrictions will be lifted and we will be able to explore again, even if that starts with just being able to go camping in Quebec. (Andrea Fraser)

It is a bad news / good news story that I share in the context of this pandemic. I lost my mother in August 2019 when she died of a stroke. Her family is grateful that she did not have to go through COVID-19 because she would surely have been a victim. Ironically, in her young years she was one of the first two known cases of typhoid fever in Toronto – she and one other person. They had no idea what it was back then. Luckily, a doctor, who had been overseas in World War I, recognized the symptoms but there was little treatment. Obviously I would not be here today had she not recovered. (Bruce Singleton)

We display in our windows rainbows that our grandchildren have drawn. (Jacques Crépeau and Ginette Arcand)

The COVID-19 pandemic is a curious moment in which human beings have an opportunity to re-orient their relational co-existence with human and non-human life (i.e., water, trees, animals, technology). This time of social distancing and isolation can be a moment to think, feel, perceive and ultimately live in new, hopeful way(s) that consider collective ethical, social, political, economic and embodied limitations. Now is a time to dream about profound transformations of systems, in which critical creative becoming(s) are possible, so that a turn towards a new era can emerge. (Mindy Carter, Associate Professor, Department of Integrated Studies in Education, McGill University)

Rainbow drawing "Ça va bien aller" by 7-year-old Lohan Arcand (photo by Daniel Arcand)

Negative feelings

We miss socializing with friends, visiting Brother Jack and Merle, cross-country skiing – now hiking – in the woods, live music (live stream is just not the same!), eating out, and grocery shopping without having to wear plastic gloves and a face mask. We've had to cancel or postpone our summer travel plans, including to Tennessee in June for Carol's Aunt Dotty's 100th birthday celebration and to France in August for the Lefebvre/Fraser family tour of Normandy. Carol very much misses singing with her quartet and elsewhere. (Jim Fraser)

Shedding a tear for COVID-19 (sketch by Jennifer Hurd)

When it was announced that schools would be closed for 2-3 weeks, I was naïve enough to shout "Oh goody, goody, I will be able to have [my great-grandchildren] Kijana and Mitsy." However, when it became evident that no such thing would happen – and that I would not get to even see them for months – I was really sad, as was Janice [my daughter, their grandmother]. Except for Janice, no one comes inside my house. I wave to them and chat from the porch. (June Patterson)

I miss being able to hug my adult children. I miss being able to work in my new job because the planned training for it was derailed by the crisis. My father-in-law Dick can't go get his hair cut, his toenails trimmed or his painful knee looked at by a doctor. (Jennifer Tracy)

Not seeing my mom has been so difficult. She lives only a seven-minute drive away. The boys and I normally see her either every day or every other day. Now, we Skype with her. On her birthday, Linden and I delivered a cake to her doorstep. We waved and blew kisses to her from the window. Later that evening, we all Skyped with Mom and Richard. We sang Happy Birthday and watched her blow out her candles from our iPad. (Tara Abramyk)

Two weeks before COVID-19 turned Canada upside-down, Phil began two new old vehicle restoration projects. Under normal circumstances, he would be spending most afternoons in his garage with our good neighbour, Bert, exploring these challenges together. Now, my disappointed man works alone, uninspired and frustrated. (Marilyn Reed)

One of the most difficult "side effects" of this pandemic has been not seeing our children and grandchildren. Until March 11, I would see them almost every day. Since then, I have not been able to hug or hold them. I have waved to them from a distance, or seen them on Skype from time to time. We have missed some things from our usual routine, too. On Friday mornings, we usually went to breakfast in Dalmeny at Granny B's. We miss her and her meals. Richard misses his Thursday evening volleyball games, which stopped in late February. We both miss our once -a-month volleyball suppers. We miss taking suppers to Richard's dad, who is 99, and we miss family gatherings. (Diane Keet)

David misses being able to go over to the Parliament Buildings to verify his material for publication. The project has been put on a back burner for the time being. (Margaret Gussow)

We worry about Brother Jack (whom we cannot visit in person), knowing that residents of retirement and nursing homes are especially vulnerable. And we know the situation must be extremely difficult for Merle. (Jim Fraser and Carol Alette)

At first, the entire pandemic really unsettled me. Nothing was the same and nothing was certain. Once I realized that life is truly always uncertain, I relaxed quite a bit. But I feel for others – so many mourning, so many laid off, so many overworked and under-protected. Personally, I am grateful. (Kerri Fraser)

For several years, as a volunteer at the Lennoxville Library, I have been spoiled. Whenever the latest novel written by a favourite author arrived, it was held for me to pick up as soon as I walked through the doors. Phil and I both devour books. But now we must wait. I also miss my much-anticipated hairdresser appointments with Rose every six weeks since many years. (Marilyn Reed)

Whenever I get a cough, I automatically think COVID-19. I have had some bouts of dry coughing for a while now. It's probably just bronchitis, but I am avoiding going to my family doctor or a hospital for fear of contracting the nasty disease while in the process of checking whether I am already infected with it! (Warren Fraser)

Since the beginning of COVID-19, I have stayed at home. Jeremy and Suraya have brought me my medications and groceries for which I am so very grateful. If I absolutely had to go out I just don't think I could. This frightens me! (Karen Jackson)

I have experienced a great deal of anxiety during this pandemic. I worry about the health of family and friends. I hope that my brother-in-law George and brother John are soon able to have loved ones visit again. I wonder when I will be able to hug my children and grandchildren again. (Diane Keet)

The two most stressful aspects of the pandemic so far for me have been: 1) witnessing and enduring the political interference with scientific knowledge and proven public health procedures, and 2) thinking that I might have the virus myself. Thankfully, I did not. That is, of course, unless my test result was a false negative. Yes, I was tested – right here in my little town of Hayfork [California]. (Sally Aldinger)

We both worry about our elderly friends, some who are in seniors' residences and/or nursing homes, and we hope and pray that they will be cared for as well as possible. We also worry about the small not-for-profit establishments and what this will mean for them in the future — only time will tell. (Sharon Moore and Royce Rand)

We miss the visits to our favorite restaurants to use our coupons/senior discounts. We miss puttering around antique and thrift shops. (Art Pease)

I miss seeing my dad as well as my kids who aren't living at home. We miss going to church and being with our "church family." Not being able to celebrate birthdays, holidays and such has been hard. It would be much harder without technology, though. (Tracie Dougherty)

Everyone, including myself, is well and has displayed no symptoms of coronavirus. So why do I feel so stressed, impatient and annoyed with everything? Because never before has one had to be limited in one's actions, shopping pattern, substitution of food items, visitation privileges, displacement and travel plans. (Lisa Taubensee)

My fears — the length of time this will last. I have two daughters who are working on the front lines. This terrifies me and I pray every day that they will be okay. I also fear for my husband, who has health issues. We will isolate, clean and do whatever is necessary to get through this pandemic. After that it will be in God's hands. (Barb Ward)

My worries are these (just asking!): What happens to my possessions and home if I die from the virus? Will a "safety crew" arrive with flame throwers to eradicate all vestiges of the virus? Will my surviving family ever be able to enter my home? (George Dunbar)

An unknown future

The heading of this section expresses a concern that everyone has. Some share their preoccupations about what the future holds. Even though it has only been a few weeks, the crisis already seems to have lasted longer than haying season at Pine Hill Farm during a rainy summer.

It is hard to imagine what will come next. No one anticipated that our world would see 90% of students out of school, although many of them learning online. No one anticipated a near complete global shutdown of businesses and the implementation of social distancing measures. It is hard to wrap our heads around what will come next and how we will begin to return to "normal." It is difficult to even understand what the new normal will be in the short, medium and long terms. (Joanne Carruthers)

As for the future, I think we are going to be in "one day at a time" mode for quite a while. With the virus reproductive rate (R0) at around 2.5, it only takes one inconsiderate or foolish person to restart the spread of the disease in a community. (Frasier Bellam)

Railway tracks at sunrise (photo by author)

While we try not to worry too much, the thoughts of "What if?" and "What next?" are always there. (Tracie Dougherty)

I hope when all this is done some things will change. I hope we will be more genuine with each other. We will take better care of the earth. We will make do with less, live more simply. Take better care of the vulnerable: seniors, poor, refugees. I hope health care policies will recognize that everyone needs to be healthy for all of us to be healthy. I hope businesses operate more efficiently with more people working from home, less airline travel for meetings. Better health care for all countries. I hope that total deaths are fewer than what we would have had during the same time period due to car, bus, train and plane accidents; mass shootings; al Qaida killings; Israeli and Palestinian killings; and abortions. I hope we will be wiser, gentler, more genuine. Towards the beginning, I removed my wedding ring to allow myself to better wash my hands. When all this is controlled, I look forward to putting the ring back on, to hugging my adult children, to sharing meals with friends and family. (Jennifer Tracy)

My worry is primarily just how much longer before there is a breakthrough and we get back to some kind of normality. My hope is for an end to this crisis with the fewest possible more deaths. (Steve Fraser)

It has not always been easy to tread the line between fear of the virus (trying to protect my friend and myself because you hate to be the one to "bring it home") and trying to keep positive, realizing there will eventually be an end. The hard part is when. Also, will a company that's been kind enough to start with me remotely, stay by me if the situation still won't allow people to go to work and move freely anytime soon? (Lisa Taubensee)

I certainly worry about the near and not too near future – more for our children and grandchildren. (George Dunbar)

I am certain that one day we shall defeat this disease or at least control it with a readily available vaccine. (Warren Fraser)

In the end it will all be okay. These interesting times always seem to work out for the better. (Lorenzo Tartamella)

We wonder what returning to the normal will be for all of us, even the youngest ones. We hope we will be able to travel once again, not just in our own province of Quebec but also to visit family in Ontario. And, we hope that our favourite travel group will soon be able to offer trips again, in particular, the one we had to cancel for September 2020 to Yorkshire and the Lake District in the U.K. (Sharon Moore and Royce Rand)

I am 75. COVID-19, plus climate change, frighten me, and I am concerned about the future for my two granddaughters. My heart is saddened. (Frank Hall)

Strategies for coping

Canada's Centre for Addiction and Mental Health offers the following strategies to help maintain one's mental wellness during the COVID-19 pandemic. The CAMH points out that some of these steps might apply to any given individual and some may not.

- Accept that some anxiety and fear is normal
- Seek credible information
- Assess your personal risk
- Find a balance: Stay tuned in, but know when to take a breather
- Bring an intentional mindset to unplugging
- Deal with problems in a structured way
- Remember that you are resilient and be careful with the "What ifs"
- Challenge worries and anxious thoughts
- Decrease other stress
- Practice relaxation and meditation
- Seek support
- Be kind to yourself
- Eat healthily
- Avoid substance use – including smoking, vaping and alcohol
- Moderate caffeine intake

Candy cane symbol of love (photo by author)

- Get proper rest and sleep
- Stay active

(source: https://www.camh.ca/en/health-info/mental-health-and-COVID-19)

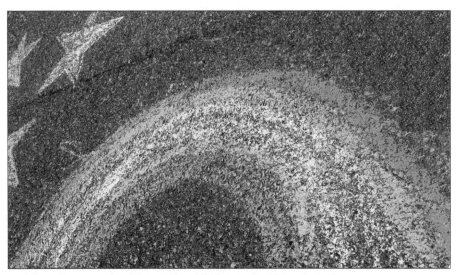

Rainbow drawn on the driveway by child (photo by Elaine Fraser)

Chapter 18
Silver linings

Cloud with a silver lining (photo by author)

Every cloud has a silver lining and the corona cumulonimbus is no exception. Amidst the pervasive darkness, there appear bright rays of encouragement. Good news stories fight to be heard through the cacophony of bad news. In this chapter, people share their own silver linings, however simple or profound they may be.

One of my own silver linings was having my hair cut by my daughter Elaine during my emergency isolation stay at her home. This was a big deal for me because it was the first time in my adult life that I didn't get sheared at Benny's barber shop in Montreal. Following is an abridged version of a piece I wrote some years ago in our family's biannual newsletter, the LINK, entitled "Benny the Barber: A Cut Above."

> There aren't many people in life who are as close to a man as is his barber. He serves not only as your hair manager, but also as your news and sports reporter, your economic advisor, your political commentator and even, at times, your psychologist. And there aren't many people in life whom you trust more than your barber. Tell me, to whom other than your barber would you submit yourself, restrained in a straitjacket, to be

operated on with an array of weapons that includes a pair of 10-inch pointy scissors and the deadly straight razor? What, then, makes a visit to the barber such a positive experience? There may be many reasons. But for me, the reason can be expressed in one word: Benny. Until he passed away (and the business was passed to his brother Mike), he was the only barber that I'd ever had. That is, apart from my mother, who clipped my locks (as well as those of my six brothers) from diaper days right up until we left the family nest.

Soon after I arrived in Montreal from the Eastern Townships in 1965, I stumbled across a rather dingy barbershop in the concourse of Central Station. Badly needing a haircut, I dropped in to check out the scene.

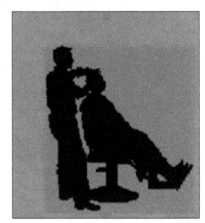

Benny the barber

Even though this was in downtown Montreal, the shop had the look of a small town barbershop rather than a big city hair salon. The décor was simple and basic: the traditional rotating barber pole at the entrance, three or four guest chairs, a table of reading material (including well-read newspapers and men's "cultural" magazines), a circular container of combs for sale on the counter, and a healthy supply of hair on the floor. A tall young man with black hair and an Italian accent welcomed me with the words: "Hello... wanna haircut?" I said, "Yes" (what else could I say!) and he pointed me in the direction of a chair with the name "Benny" behind it. A moment of fear gripped me as I climbed into the big leather chair with padded armrests. The chair's similarity to that of the dreaded dentist chair gave me some rather scary flashbacks. Nonetheless, I bravely settled into the chair for a totally new experience in my life.

When Benny threw the silky sheet around me and tied it tightly around my neck, I knew that I had reached the point of no return. As I silently contemplated the ordeal that was about to unfold, Benny broke the silence with a question for which I was quite unprepared. "How would you like it?" he asked. My first thought was to point to one of the photos on the wall and say "Like him." But because my current hair "style" did not even remotely resemble any of those pictured, I didn't dare take the chance. After a brief pause, I said something like "Oh, just leave it the same as it is now . . ." Interpreting my answer, he replied: "OK, same style but a bit shorter . . . right?" I agreed and proceeded to experience my first formal haircut at the age of 21. I came out of that first experience in fine shape without so much as a nick above the ear. Benny had won my confidence and I was ready to take him on as my permanent barber. (Winston Fraser)

Another of my own silver linings is sports-related. As a long-time Montreal Canadiens supporter, I have been very disappointed with their lamentable lack of success in recent years. It was obvious that, even though they hadn't yet been mathematically eliminated, they would miss the playoffs again this year. So the suspension of the NHL schedule saved the Habs from the ignominious embarrassment of missing the post-season once again!

Many of those who contributed to this book have shared the silver linings they have experienced in the midst of these challenging times:

Having lots of time on my hands, I have had the opportunity to take walks along the Lakeshore, to slow down and observe the happenings around me. The snow has disappeared, birds and geese have appeared and there are days when I can close my eyes and pretend that I'm at the ocean listening to the waves roll in. The birds are so talkative on the sunny early mornings – they bring hope. I have noticed how quiet the surroundings have become – fewer vehicles on the highway and very few planes landing and taking off. I've enjoyed a few walks in the rain with heavy fog hanging over the water. The fog was so thick that you couldn't see across the water or even along the shoreline to spot the high-rises which you can usually see. It was sort of an eerie feeling – especially when it looked like the fog was rising like steam out of a large cauldron. In fact, the view made me think of the three witches brewing a potion in Macbeth – "Double, double, toil and trouble; Fire burn, and cauldron bubble . . ." I must admit I prefer walking early in the morning, at night or in bad weather so that there are not lots of other people, from whom I need to social distance, thus detracting from the peace of walking. (Monique Thirlwell)

Walking in fog and rain (photo by Monique Thirlwell)

My silver lining was having Dad live with us during my sister's and brother-in-law's 14-day travel isolation. It brought me such happiness to provide a "space" for him. Although in strange and uncertain circumstances, it was a time that I will always hold dear. Scrabble nights, morning chats in the living room, walks along the Lakeshore, Buddy-dog love, etc. It was not a "normal" time and still isn't but it helped give me and our family a focus – take care of Dad and keep Bubba safe. (Elaine "Fuzzy" Fraser)

Buddy rests on his personal bench, Dorval, Que. (photo by author)

Our "Tupperware" drawer stays tidy since we're not making and taking away three lunches every day. (Jennifer Tracy)

We have started to write a daily journal of our activities, impressions and other information, including that related to the pandemic. The pandemic will have a before and an after. We will remember it and our descendants will refer to it just as we refer to the Spanish flu that we did not experience. A review of the burial records of our local Saint-David d'Yamaska parish showed that in October 1918 alone, 17 persons (aged between 1 and 40 years) died of the flu. (Jacques Crépeau and Ginette Arcand)

I have an additional silver lining to mention. TSN is now showing some old Montreal Expos baseball games, probably because currently no sports are being played. I am watching these games and reliving the experience of attending some of those games at the Big O in Montreal. It is truly uplifting for me at this very crazy time in our lives. (Karen Jackson)

Our silver lining is getting caught up on things to do in the house. (David and Margaret Gussow)

We have seen a big decrease in the amount of money spent on shopping and impulse buying. (Tracie Dougherty)

I have never slept so well. Our house is very close to the sidewalk and often there would be groups of loud, noisy people making their way home from the pub. Now, with the pub closed, there is only silence. Also, I am finally using up things in the freezer that I didn't know I had. (Margaret Eastwood)

In retirement, I became an avid book reader and during these past few weeks even more so. It is a marvelous pastime. (Steve Fraser)

(1) We had hired an architect to design an expansion to our weekend home for when we retire and move here full-time. After living here (and not leaving the house very often), we realized we don't need nearly the space we thought we did. Like so many others, our retirement accounts have taken a beating, so we have been rethinking the renovation, reducing its size and eliminating some of the more costly features. And despite the lack of social interaction and limited recreation activities, we realized that this is truly where we want to live.

(2) The leadership of my firm has been talking about a distributed workforce for several years as we look to hire the best people no matter where they are located and to address long commutes and the high price of real estate in urban centers. When and if we get back to normal, whatever that looks like, I imagine we will look at office space and location differently.

(3) Finally, I have realized how fortunate I am to be stuck in paradise with Sean, that our children have wonderful partners to help them get through this, and that we are able to stay connected with all our family and friends thorough this challenging time. (Pat Tracy-Callahan)

We both are realizing that, without the usual demands of our volunteer work, there is time to do our own spring cleaning in garage/workshop and house. Sorting and discarding (downsizing?) is happening, and by taking it gradually we are not finding the time long or boring. We both try to have something for the morning and something else for the afternoon. Old files are finally getting shredded, cupboards sorted and rearranged with some things being boxed up with the hope that garage sales will happen once again. Evenings are free from meetings, allowing us to watch television together. (Sharon Moore and Royce Rand)

One final silver lining from me: I believe that this pandemic has highlighted the abominable conditions of some of Canada's First Nations communities and caused the government to allocate significant funds to help alleviate their plight.

A friend named Betty saw her dark cloud of grieving transformed into a silver lining of gratitude and giving. She shares her story entitled "The 3 G's of COVID-19:"

As we shelter in place, our individual worlds have become smaller. Mine is a 943-square-foot one-bedroom apartment. During this time of enforced isolation, I felt that I needed a plan to redefine my world. I knew that there were many things I could not control in the outside world. Yet the collective grief we all feel is affected by it. We all grieve for those who are suffering, the families of those who have died, those who are lonely or depressed, the many who are hungry and without income. That part of the world, I cover by prayer.

For the small world that I can control, I knew I needed some type of plan. It is only me. I know from experience that not dealing with grief, affects mental and physical health. So the first G is to list things when I grieve. In black and white, they cannot be ignored. But how to counteract this cloud of grief? That would take giving thanks for all that I do have (G #2) and to do my best to give away what I could (G #3). An attitude of gratitude does wonders for a down day. So does thinking of creative ways to give back and make a difference in the world.

G #1: Grieving

- It hurts each time I throw out a can or paper or other things that were recycled in other times. For decades, I've conscientiously separated and recycled whatever was appropriate. And the redeemable bottles and cans were given to the church. It hurts that I don't have enough space to store these items until this is over.
- I miss the sunshine. This smaller apartment is not facing the light. No herbs will grow on the patio. No light greets or ends the day. It is dark. Thank goodness for my SAD light.
- As much as I appreciate my "alone time," I miss the freedom of going where I want to go, when I want to go. Someone else shops, drives and delivers what I need. I miss the process of going there myself.
- I miss in-person meetings, coffee and happy hours, lunches in person with my friends. These always began with a hug. No more hugs.
- The memory of hearing live symphony music is beginning to fade. My music now comes through tiny speakers.
- I am sad not to be able to start my business as planned. I could have helped many people and my bank account as well. We make plans, God laughs.

G #2: Gratitude

- Every time I take a hot shower, I give thanks. As the water streams over me, I visualize the worries of the day washing down the drain. When washing my hands, I take longer. So I do the same in the shower and appreciate coming out clean and fresh.
- Bless the shoppers and delivery people who bring fresh food to me so I can shelter safely.
- Amazon Pantry is amazing. While they may no longer be immediate, they get the job done.
- My Girl Scout training – Be Prepared. It helped fuel the planner in me to have a stocked pantry, protective items for emergencies and the comfort in the knowledge that I have enough.
- My dreams. I dream of shopping at the local supermarket, shelves full of all the brands that I love. I dream of Happy Hours and Coffee Hours where I can touch the arm of my friends. LOTS of hugs. My dreams take me to places I cannot go at the moment and this gives me comfort.
- I never would believe that I'd be praising technology. Yet today I give thanks for the ease by which we remain connected. Church services, dance parties, meetings, happy hours and just visual chats.
- I'm thankful that I know how to exist happily on my own. Loneliness is something I very seldom feel. I'm used to choosing to spend time with myself.
- My apartment is as tidy or messy, as sterile or in need of vacuuming as I wish. No need to have it "presentable" for others who might come over. That said, I have to have organization to be sane. But when I have a project, I can leave it out until completion. No one will see.
- Grateful for my regular government cheques. They are automatically

deposited and come on schedule, as promised.

G #3: Giving

- Donating my stock of hundreds of masks and gloves to the local hospital workers, with 12 thank-you cards to those on the front lines.
- Answering the call to help the local transitional home for veterans after their fire.
- Donating to my church's food pantry.
- Hand writing thank-you notes to the cleaning and maintenance workers here at the apartment complex.
- Donating my tickets back to the theater when the performances were cancelled.
- Verbal thanks to my local grocer and pharmacy were much appreciated when I spoke with them.
- Buying groceries for a neighbour in my final trip to the store, weeks ago.
- Sending my last two masks to my BFF who is still shopping for food in a hot spot of the virus.
- Thanking the credit card company representative was very well received.
- Leaving a thank you note for mailman, John, for all he does for us.
- Calling my new friend "Debbie Downer." It is a hard balance to be supportive without being affected by her negativity. I don't advise. I just try to be an example to someone who is very unhappy and living in total fear.

That is my story. (Betty Maine)

My California cousin Sally's silver lining was receiving the good news that she did NOT have the COVID-19 virus after being a suspected positive case. Here is her fascinating story:

My daughter Sarah had an event in San Diego at the end of February and took my granddaughter Abigail with her on a five-day trip to visit all the sites. They flew in an airplane, stayed in a hotel and ate in restaurants. Abigail was quite ill with a high fever and cough the day after they returned. Then Sarah fell sick with a high fever, which resolved after three days. But Abigail's cough persisted and her fever relapsed. In the meantime, I became sick with a high fever for four days. Sarah called our local clinic to take Abigail in. They were met in a special parking area by people fully garbed in PPE who gave them each an N95 mask to put on. They listened to Abigail's lungs, and because her fever was down and no sign of pneumonia was detected, they sent her home.

While at the clinic, Sarah mentioned that I was also sick, and was told to have me call in to be seen, which I did and was also met in the special parking area and given a mask to put on. I was led through the back door of the clinic into the back room, met by a PA (Physician's Assistant). She heard my story, took my temperature, listened to my lungs, and did the

COVID-19 test by swabbing my throat and my nose (ouch!). While listening to my lungs, she heard a rattle in the left lung, which I could also hear – it sounded to me like creaking old floor boards. That triggered me

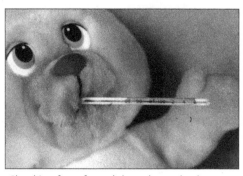

needing to complete Advanced Directives with a sterilized pen, and a trip to Trinity Hospital in Weaverville. I was met in the parking lot by someone in PPE who escorted me through the back door to the x-ray room. I was told that a radiologist in Redding would review the x-ray and send the results to Hayfork Clinic. That was a Friday morning, so I had to wait out the weekend for the results of both the x-ray and the COVID-19 test. I was told to go home and stay home, and that I would be contacted by either someone from the clinic or by a public health nurse.

Checking for a fever (photo by author)

During that two-day wait for what turned out to be negative results, I had time to think about many things, including whether my affairs were in order, what are all the passwords were that my daughter will need to know, where the key to the safety deposit box was located, and most of all, whether they would be okay without me. I cried just once in thinking

Cloud with a silver lining (photo by author)

about maybe having to leave them, first, if I were hospitalized in Redding, or worse, if I did not recover. Then I decided to banish those grim thoughts, and managed to muster the energy to do the laundry and get a few things organized – just in case. Tomorrow, I will have been staying at home for exactly one month. Not only are we all under orders from our California Governor Gavin Newsom, but I am conscious that it could have been a false negative test. My energy is starting to return, I have no more fevers, and I am able to do more each day. Sarah and Abigail have visited in the yard, and the beautiful spring days are providing the best medicine. (Sally Aldinger)

Chapter 19
Return to normalcy

"Is the war over yet?" (sketch by James Harvey)

Obviously, the whole story of COVID-19 has not yet been written, and that I will leave to others. But the dreaded "peak" appears to have passed and we are assured that better times are ahead.

At the time of going to press, there are positive signs of light at the end of the tunnel. Some businesses have started to reopen. On April 14 Quebec redefined "essential" services, adding new industries to its list of essential services and businesses that can remain open during the province's lockdown. Some residential construction, mines, auto mechanics, and gardening centres will be allowed to reopen. And on April 27 the Quebec government announced the reopening of elementary schools on May 11. However, on May 16 the government announced that schools in the Montreal area will remain closed until at least September.

The complete return to the old normal will be a long process. Indeed it may not ever happen. Instead, we may have to accept a new normal, whatever form it may take.

Epilogue

Although I have written several books over the past few years, the experience of putting this one together has been very different from all the others.

For starters, the subject matter was completely outside of my area of expertise. Having previously concentrated on historical biographies and photographic coffee-table books, the medical/pandemic field was absolutely foreign to me. I have had to learn a whole new jargon – from PPE to "planking the curve."

Secondly, the conditions under which I wrote were quite unique. Not only was I in self-isolation the whole time, but the sands were constantly shifting under me as new and updated information became available on a daily – sometimes hourly – basis.

Another significant difference was the compressed time frame in which I completed this book. On my earlier publishing endeavours, I spent an average of almost 12 months from start to finish. For this one, it took only two months, including 24 days of actual "nose to the keyboard" writing.

Perhaps the greatest difference of all was that I felt an urgency that I had never sensed before. As mentioned in the Preface, I was determined to finish the book before the crisis had ended and normalcy had returned. In retrospect, maybe I needn't have been in such a hurry, because it doesn't appear that normalcy will happen anytime soon.

In closing, I hope that this book has both informed and inspired you. And I pray that it has helped you to appreciate those blessings that we may too often have taken for granted.

I urge you once more to stay safe, stay healthy and stay connected.

Winston

CPSIA information can be obtained
at www.ICGtesting.com
Printed in the USA
LVHW021232240820
663959LV00038B/1628